Begin with Yes:

Nighttime Affirmations

Dream with intention

By Paul S. Boynton

ISBN: 0-9981718-1-6

ISBN-13: 978-0-9981718-1-4

Published by: Toby Dog Media

Cover photos by: Benjamin Williamson
Website: www. benjaminwilliamsonphotography.com

Dedication

For Toby Dog.

You make two guys very happy!

Forward

When Paul first approached me about writing the introduction to this book, I must say, I was flattered. I've known Paul for a few years and have worked on other projects with him; I know the caliber of his work and the truths in what he says. On a personal level, I also know what a genuine and authentic person he is. In short, he walks his talk. And these days, that's a somewhat rare and beautiful thing to find in a person. So, when he asked me to write this, I had a feeling of, "Gosh, little ol' me? He wants *me* to write it? That's so flattering." It wasn't false modesty, but more along the lines of wondering why he'd ask me when he knows so many other interesting people.

Then I realized what a ridiculous crock that was, and how much it goes against everything Paul says about being true to ourselves and living an authentic life and taking steps and appreciating each step as part of the journey. After all, isn't this the type of thing I've been working toward? Haven't I busted my butt to have my work noticed and appreciated, and to have my own voice heard in the crowd? Yes, it is, and yes, I have.

That is also a perfect example of how gentle, often subtle, and yet, how profound Paul's influence and words are. I find myself paying attention even when I think I'm not. I find myself absorbing the simplicity of what he says and applying it to intricacies in my life without even realizing, until afterwards, that that's what I've done. In fact, it took me a long time to edit this book for him and part of that was because I'd find myself reading through Paul's words and then pausing to take in what I'd just read. I'd lean back, sip my coffee, and think, "Huh. Wow. That's... wow." That's saying a lot for a woman who generally rolls her eyes and nods off at the mere mention of non-fiction (unless it's a really fascinating historical piece). All this is to say that I've changed my stance. I am no longer flattered, but I am deeply honored. I am honored because I have listened to Paul's words. I have applied them to my life.

And now I'm seeing the fruit of the work I've been doing for the past five or so years. To have that recognized is, absolutely, an honor.

As we were talking about the editing process, Paul mentioned what he wanted to use as the working title of this book. I think my immediate response was, "Oh! I love that!" *Second Star to the Right** comes from J.M. Barrie's classic children's book, *Peter Pan*. "Second start to the right, and straight on 'til morning!" is spoken by Peter Pan as he is giving directions for reaching Neverland to the Darling children who have just learned to fly. It fits with this book on many levels. Paul's joy, unadulterated enthusiasm, and sense of adventure are much like those found in the character of Peter Pan. He doesn't worry about whether or not we're able to fly; he trusts that we already are flying and simply points out the direction.

Paul, just like Peter Pan, wants everybody to be part of the experience. Even more, he wants us to have our own experience. Then he deftly lays out guidelines for making the most of the experience, all the while bolstering the enthusiasm of those around him. Although this is real life for us, and not a fairy tale, we begin to realize that anything really is possible. Magic and miracles do happen. Dreams can come true. All it takes is us, individually and together, believing and working until the impossible is more than possible, it's our reality.

As you read each evening's affirmation, you'll find yourself further along on a tremendous adventure - the adventure of you. And, oh, but you'll love the night breeze as you glide on towards morning.

Barb Black

* Although the title was changed to Begin with Yes – Nighttime Affirmations, the magic remains the same. PSB

Introduction

I hope you'll keep this book on your bedside table, ready and waiting for you each night as you go to sleep. You'll be joining people from all over the world who are making "nighttime affirmations" part of their bedtime routine. Although it was created in the format of a calendar to be read night by night, you can also simply open the book to a random page and date and discover a powerful thought that will connect with you at "that perfect time".

And remember, the power is not in the words, but rather in the ideas, feelings and thoughts the words evoke for you. The power lies in your desire to take your dreams seriously and to follow your passions wherever they take you. Most of all, these words are here to remind you that although you weren't given wings to fly, you were given dreams to soar.

With love and high hope for each one of us, "Sleep tight".

Paul S. Boynton

January

January 1

With each step forward, we are becoming who we already are, who we have always been and who we were always meant to be. It's such a privilege to be sharing this journey with you. Rest well.

January 2

Self-responsibility and self-esteem seem to go hand-in-hand. The more you have of one, the more you have of the other. And taking small steps sets it all in motion. Before you go to sleep tonight, decide which step you'll take tomorrow, and you'll fall asleep with a plan and a smile.

January 3

When we take small, consistent steps towards what "could be", we are actually joining force with the Universe to co-create what "will be". If we aren't willing to look beyond our current situations, we will miss incredible opportunities to create new realities! And just because it can sometimes be a challenge to do that, it doesn't mean we can't do that. Tonight, focus on the possibilities and get some good rest!

January 4

When it feels like you have the weight of the world on your shoulders, it's time to let go of some serious baggage. For starters, let go of responsibilities that belong to others. Let go of things beyond your control. Let go of past mistakes. Let go of regrets. Let go. Let go. Let go. Lighter. Lighter. Lighter. Turn worried thoughts into hopeful ones as you fall asleep. Rest well!

January 5

Peace and contentment exist in that space between seeking important things that will nourish our hearts, minds and souls, and recognizing and deeply appreciating the things in our lives that already do. The power of our collective steps is that of many rivers and streams converging toward a beautiful waterfall. Not only are we changing *our* world, we are changing *the* world! Let that put a smile on your face as you head to sleep.

January 6

To continue growing we need to be intimately connected with others and intimately connected with ourselves. One very simple but amazing way to become more connected to others is to listen to and affirm their heart songs. Getting ready to sleep is a wonderful time to practice listening to and affirming your own. Wishing you amazing dreams tonight.

January 7

You may not be perfect. The day may not have been perfect. Your life may not be perfect. The world may not be perfect. But that doesn't mean they aren't each perfectly beautiful. Rest well beautiful!

January 8

Dream big. Welcome bedtime as recovery time for your body and mind, and dreaming as discovery time for your heart.

January 9

"We need to learn the difference between having a willingness to be kind, open and forgiving and being a doormat. One allows us to maintain our dignity and self-respect and the other leaves us with a pit in the stomach. Once you know the difference, your behavior will change forever!" – *Paul Boynton "Begin with Yes"*

Let go of any thoughts that will keep you from resting peacefully. You can always reclaim them tomorrow in the light of day.

January 10

The response to darkness is your compassion, your kindness, your love and the very light of your heart and soul. As dark as it may get, always remember that you are of the light and the light will always, always prevail.

January 11

Sometimes all we can do and what we are called to do is to silently stand beside someone who is grieving and let them know we understand and care, not with our words but with a gentle touch. When your head finally hits the pillow tonight, think about the smiles of the people you love, those nearby, those far away, and those who are sweet and beautiful memories that will stay with you forever. Remembering each smile is a way to count your blessings and invites sleep to gently find you.

January 12

Tonight, be in touch with your innocence - the deeper, more authentic you where all the hurts and disappointments, all the mistakes, regrets and wrong turns are pushed aside - where the real you emerges once again. Then welcome home and celebrate the beautiful, innocent, complete and deserving person simply here to create, to share, and to love and be loved. You are so much stronger and so much more capable than you may feel in this moment. If you don't believe me, just look at all you've already dealt with and remind yourself – you're still here! Rest easy tonight!

January 13

Tonight, lovingly and with a smile remember someone dear to you who has passed on… Imagine that they have something very meaningful and helpful to share with you. As you get ready to sleep, close your eyes, open your heart and quietly listen. Rest gently and see what you learn.

January 14

As the night lights appear, think of one person in your life who may be feeling scared or discouraged, or who is dealing with a challenge, and make a phone call or send a quick note of encouragement. Not only will one night be changed for one person, but the ripples will expand out into the world. And as your day winds down, you'll be able to smile to yourself, knowing you made a difference. Rest.

January 15

Some days are easier than others. But no matter how today went for you, rest gently tonight, while looking forward to another day and another chance to take a step or two in the direction of your heart's desire. It's okay to be fearful and tentative, just as long as you keep moving forward! Remember even the smallest of steps count big! Sleep tight.

January 16

Often our instinct is to resist change. It never actually works – in fact, it usually makes our progress so much more difficult. Maybe it's time to try resisting less and risking more.

January 17

Obviously, we are called to love, help and encourage others. However, one common mistake is that we try to make someone else (or everyone else) happy. It just can't be done. Instead we need to turn our attention and energy toward our own goals and dreams - things that we feel passion for. By doing that, we show others how to seek happiness for themselves. Rest well tonight.

January 18

One step at time can sometimes be measured in minutes. One less minute today spent worrying is a goal every single one of us could achieve. If we take that minute of worry and replace it with a minute spent thinking peaceful, loving thoughts, those minutes will add up. Slowly our minds and our realities will begin to shift in wonderful ways. Getting ready to sleep is the perfect time to practice.

January 19

Say this out loud to yourself. "Tonight, as I move toward sleep, I gently lay my ideas, worries, fears, plans, hopes and thoughts about tomorrow on the bedside table. I take a few deep and slow breaths, and welcome the blanket of love and safety that surrounds me. As I drift off to dreams, I trust that everything can rest until a new beginning tomorrow."

January 20

Take comfort knowing that although we may be in different cars, we are all on the same train. And we are all actually heading up the same mountain.

January 21

When we lose someone we love, we discover that time does not heal everything. After a while, the ache in our heart begins to ease a bit, and we laugh again. Life goes on and many times we reconnect with those still physically with us in much deeper more beautiful ways. Eventually the good memories outnumber the sad thoughts and we begin to sense that what we thought was lost has actually been with us all along. We can't explain it, touch it or prove it – but there are moments we catch ourselves smiling because we know it's true.

January 22

Although there are many paths up the mountain, one small step is the only way to begin the climb. Always remember, you are not alone and there will be help along the way. By choosing love even when you're struggling, even when your heart is breaking, even when your challenges seem almost more than you can bear, you are choosing power and hope. And power and hope will hold you steady thru the difficult days and gently lift you into calmer waters. You are beautiful and worthy of respect and hope no matter how you're feeling.

January 23

As you remember the people you love, also remember that we're falling asleep sharing tonight's sky. Most of the really interesting, compassionate and influential people in the world have faced major disappointments, have had their hearts broken once or twice, have heard and marched to that different drum, and have experienced loneliness, despair and failure. Not surprisingly, these same people create beautiful art, music, dance and theatre, and become deeply intuitive, generous and unconditional lovers.

January 24

Imagine a low tide that never became high tide. Or a night that never shifted towards morning. And imagine important goals never being reached and dreams never coming true. Ridiculous, I know. If you look, you will notice miracles tonight.

January 25

Having deep and intimate relationships can add new meaning and beauty to our lives and it is wonderful to love and be loved and to cherish and be cherished. But always remember that you, all by yourself, are enough. You are complete, beautiful and whole. And with that as your starting place, you move forward not waiting for but fully expecting that you will draw other healthy, happy, complete people into your lives to share parts of the journey.

January 26

You will never have all the answers because each answer creates new questions. There's a sweet rhythm here when you remember that one question, one answer, one step at a time is how life is meant to unfold... kind of like breathing while you're asleep.

January 27

When did we stop wanting to hear lullabies? When did we stop needing to hear gentle, comforting words as the day comes to a close? When did we stop saying simple prayers of gratitude as we settled into our beds for the night? Think of this note as turn down service, a piece of chocolate on your pillow and a kiss on your forehead! Sleep tight.

January 28

The love of family and friends, and romantic love are wonderful miracles in our lives. But we can't make someone love us. Trying is a heartbreaking and a terrible waste of time, energy and self-respect. We may love someone who doesn't love us back or love us the way we want. We must let that be and move on. We may wish to be loved by someone who can only love us on their terms and only when we appear to be who they wish we were. We must let that be and move on. We may think we need a specific person to love us a certain way, but who and how others love is not up to us to decide. We must let that be and move on.

January 29

Be afraid, but don't be stopped. Be confused, but don't be stuck. Be worn out, but don't give up. You've done it before, and you can do it again. Then, when you get under the covers tonight, put it all aside, close your eyes, and open your heart so the Universe can restore and heal and get you ready for another day!

January 30

It is time to love, appreciate and accept yourself as you are and where you are right at this very moment. And it is time to love, appreciate and accept yourself for where you are headed. You are worthy and lovable from this moment on. Put your worries aside now and sleep well. Let the blessings of the new day find you rested and ready to go.

January 31

We may have a thousand steps ahead of us but if we put one or two behind us tonight, we can go to bed that much closer to our dreams. Sleep is meant to restore our dreams and our energy.

February

February 1

Head in the clouds and feet on the ground makes a perfect combination. With our minds, we create impossible and beautiful dreams, and with our feet, we take small, but confident steps toward making sure those dreams come true. Only when we remember the challenges we've faced - the obstacles, the hurt, the heartbreak, fears and disappointments we have endured - do we begin to understand the power of resiliency. We've got it and the proof is that we're still here. Now get some well-deserved rest!

February 2

If you've been drifting without a clear picture of your purpose, it's time to become more intentional. Begin by rediscovering your passions – often the things you were drawn to as a child, or things you'd be doing if life hadn't gotten in the way. Then find very small steps that enliven these thoughts or dreams. If you always wanted to be a writer, get a notebook and begin writing. If you wanted to be a veterinarian, offer to volunteer at an animal shelter. As you begin taking those small steps, a purpose will gradually reveal itself and the path will appear. That is how dreams come true.

February 3

Anger energy, especially when it's prolonged, needs to be redeployed. If you're going to maximize your potential, you can't waste a lot of energy being mad. Instead, use your energy to make something good happen! We are each vulnerable and each have the capacity to help others during difficult times. That, quite simply is why we are blessed to be on this journey together. May a sense of calm and peace surround you as you fall asleep tonight.

February 4

Practice using fear to your advantage. Don't let it paralyze you; let it motivate you instead. Because being scared isn't the problem; letting it stop you is. When you decide what's possible; you're either expanding or limiting your potential and your power. Tonight, fall to sleep thinking and dreaming expansive thoughts, and tomorrow you will wake up focused on all the amazing possibilities. Peace.

February 5

The things that have hurt you, broken your heart, made you cry with pain, grief and even rage are the very same things that have made you more human, more compassionate, and more able to help lift others into the light of unconditional love. And that's the one thing we all desperately need and the most significant, life changing gift we can offer. Love is the most powerful emotion we know – it brings us to the heights of bliss and joy and also to the depths of grief and pain. And the love we have for the animals we have adopted and who have become family, brings us this same joy and happiness, and then with illness and loss, the same confusion and pain. My thoughts tonight are with those who know this love.

February 6

Sometimes it's difficult to believe in our dreams and even more so to believe in ourselves. We push forward anyway, knowing that wanting to believe is enough to get us started, and that one day soon, we'll discover that our courage and tenacity to keep moving forward has actually nurtured our self-confidence. Then we find the steps getting bolder and more frequent because we do, after all, believe. When you begin to judge yourself less and love yourself more, you will begin to judge others less and love them more too! So tonight as you fall asleep, no self-judgments allowed.

February 7

We almost never know when we are on the verge of a breakthrough, but if we're taking risks, taking steps and staying hopeful, there's a very good chance that one is near. The challenges, struggles and difficult days are part of every journey and are always present when you're undertaking something important. They are especially predictable when you're letting go of the status quo and getting ready for something new. Fortunately, the difficult days are numbered. So, tonight, why not fall asleep looking forward to those easier, lighter, magical days ahead because they're part of the journey too.

February 8

Self-responsibility and self-esteem seem to go hand-in-hand. The more you have of one, the more you have of the other. Given that, a step taken in either direction is guaranteed to create positive momentum and immediately enhance your life. It's not too late to make today count. The world needs your light now more than ever. So, rest up – tomorrow will be here soon enough!

February 9

We are each like a magnificent tree - expansive and deep. Our branches and leaves grow toward the light: evolving, reaching, unfolding and becoming. Our deep roots ground us, holding us steady, connecting us in a solid, reliable and reassuring way. We may forget this but forgetting never changes who we are. Rest gently and dream peacefully tonight.

February 10

Tonight as you move toward sleep, gently put your ideas, worries, fears, plans, hopes and thoughts about tomorrow on the bedside table. Then take a few deep and slow breathes and welcome in the blanket of love and safety that surrounds you. As you drift off to dream, know that everything can wait until a new beginning tomorrow. Peace.

February 11

I am a great believer in "signs" that help us find our way, but I've learned that we increase the likelihood of spotting them when we're actually moving down a path – when we're not waiting, but expecting. Believing in our dreams and doing something about them are two very important and very different concepts. Tonight let's dream about doing and then wake up tomorrow ready to begin the doing.

February 12

Since it's impossible to meet all the expectations of others and be all things to all people (which takes a lot of energy), why not stay focused on your dreams. So often the people who discourage us the most from being ourselves and pursuing our dreams are the very same people who are most afraid to be themselves and to follow their own heart. Show them how it's done, and don't let them discourage you from following your dreams.

February 13

This year let's shake things up a bit and make Valentine's Day all about love in all its forms, shapes and sizes. Let's think bigger than just romance and include our family, our friends, and co-workers too. And why stop there? Let's get carried away and include the people we see in the elevator, at the coffee shop, and even strangers we pass on the street. In fact, let's make the sky the limit and smile, "Happy Valentine's Day" to every single person on our path. Love matters and you have plenty to share! Let's choose love as our theme tonight, tomorrow and forever, and change the world starting right now!

February 14

We have yearned to be loved and been afraid to love. We have experienced love that hurts and love that heals. We have been loved with many conditions and loved with no strings attached. We have loved and lost people who meant the world to us, and we have forgotten some we thought we'd love forever. We have experienced romantic love, lustful love and sometimes both. We have felt love that confused us and love that seemed to clarify everything. We've known the love of family and or friends, and we have loved our pets and been loved back just as surely as night turns to morning. We are learning by doing and although we have learned so much, we still have so much more to learn. And so we embrace love in all its many forms knowing it is our purpose, our greatest blessing and most importantly our very heart's desire. Drift to sleep tonight knowing you love and are loved.

February 15

You probably have a long list of things to remember and get done. If you don't take at least one small step towards a personal goal or dream each day, you will have missed a once in a lifetime opportunity. Small steps happen because we make them a priority. But, who hasn't missed a few opportunities and screwed up others? Most of us would also admit a few regrets and sad edges around a relationship or two. We've disappointed family, friends and even more often ourselves. Some of us have complained, whined, and been loud and then other times we've been quiet when we should have spoken up. But tonight we put all that aside, smiling at our humanness and knowing tomorrow we will have another chance.

February 16

Sometimes the smallest of actions become those pivotal and significant life changing moments. That truth alone, makes taking another small step easier and worth the effort. No matter how today went, there's a very good chance you did the best you could. The maple sugaring season will soon begin here in New Hampshire and that means that Spring is closer than we ever could have imagined during the last big snow storm. Tonight, I'm taking that as an important life lesson!

February 17

Sometimes doing our best means we got out of bed. It means that despite the realities and challenges in our path, we still managed to put one foot in front of the other and move in the direction that made the most sense for now. And it means whether today was an easy or difficult day, we remembered to be gentle, forgiving and loving with ourselves and also with those around us who are doing their best too.

February 18

Although we are far from perfect, there are some things that we do extraordinarily well. We have figured out that time and space are irrelevant as we encourage and comfort one another in meaningful, beautiful ways. What we do here is incredibly powerful, changes lives and proves, beyond any doubt, that compassion is universal and love has no boundaries. Accept today as it was and yourself as you were and rest easy.

February 19

Sometimes there are people in our lives who seem to have pressed the self-destruct button, they make one bad decision after another and seem to create chaos and heartbreak all around. We really do love them but we cannot help them. and that's a frustrating and sad place to be. So, we begin to emotionally and often even physically love them from a distance. We let go so that we can share our light and love with those who are able to receive it. And we let go so that the love and light that surrounds us can be received. When you're gentle with yourself, you'll be gentle with others. When you're non-judgmental with yourself, you'll be non-judgmental with others. When you give yourself the benefit of the doubt, you'll be able to do the same for the people around you too.

February 20

Respect and celebrate the small steps that others are taking. Walking into a room full of strangers, going to the gym, talking to a college counselor are easy for some and an incredible act of courage for others. Now, in that same spirit, respect and celebrate your own small, courageous steps too. Don't worry so much about finding yourself. Instead put your energy into creating yourself. Then rest easy tonight knowing you were there all along!

February 21

In the still of the night you will often hear the distant music of your heart. You are not your worries, your fears, your anxieties or your disappointments. You are the tender touch, helping hand and gentle smile. Being clever is not nearly as important as being kind. You are here to stand up and speak out demanding fairness, opportunity and hope. You are here on purpose and with purpose. You have everything you need and the world is waiting. The simple truth about loneliness: You can sit alone in the dark or you can get up, turn on the light, open the door and invite a friend or two in! We are counting on you and it is time to begin.

February 22

Doing our best doesn't mean we don't make mistakes. It doesn't mean that we are perfect or that everything works out the way we want in the time frame we were planning. It doesn't mean that we don't have disappointments or that we are always smiling, always hopeful or always energized with a positive spirit. What it does mean is we know how to pick ourselves up and dust ourselves off and we keep moving one small step at a time! For now, rest safely in the harbor of your dreams tonight.

February 23

Faith is an incredibly powerful tool as we step into and even welcome the mystery ahead. We don't always step into the unknown with self-confidence or lack of fear. In fact, sometimes we can barely breathe and our hands are trembling. But we do step out with a sense of self-respect, courage and belief that we deserve more. As we move into the mystery, we discover that our courage, our faith and our self-awareness deepens with every single step we take. As you get ready to sleep, breathe out worries large and small and then breathe in peace and calm. Pause. And then repeat. After three or four breaths you will actually begin to feel better and rest will come easier. Good Night.

February 24

As the evening unfolds, take a moment to remember the good things already in your life. Then with arms and heart open wide, gently move into rest. As thoughts drift into your mind, carefully sort them. Those that are worthy and helpful, keep, and move aside and forget those that are unworthy and hurtful. At the end of the day remember that love takes many forms but always illuminates the best we have to share and gives us hope for what waits for us tomorrow.

February 25

Deep within each of us there is a very specific life purpose. This truth can be ignored for a while but like a phone that keeps ringing, it won't be denied forever. Have you answer your call? Are you frustrated or angry with someone who is trying to manage your life for you? If so, I don't blame you – after all, that's your job! Sometimes a gentle reminder is all it takes. Other times you need to come right out and say it more forcefully. Of course some people will be relieved, and others will resist. Either way your job is to focus on your own life and keep moving forward. Drift gently tonight.

February 26

Do you remember the last time you were content, at peace, relaxed, safe and calm? Where were you? Can you remember the smells, the colors, the sounds and who you were with? Tonight when you get into bed, paint the picture of that memory in your mind, hug your pillow and fall asleep with a smile.

February 27

If and when we discover that our "helping" someone isn't helping, it's time redirect our energy! We each have the potential to love and change the world in ways well beyond anything we could ever imagine. But the simple truth is that this won't happen unless we honor our passions and embrace the unique and beautiful person each of us are. So, begin there and then help others honor and embrace their own passions too. Not only will your world change but the world will change too.

February 28

Practice sending quick, silent prayers or good thoughts to people around you. It can't hurt and there's a very good chance it will help! Tonight, as you fall asleep, whisper YES to your own dreams.

March

March 1

Each morning we wake up and are handed the gift of a new day, a fresh start and a chance to begin again. It's what we do with this gift that counts. No matter how today went, there's a very good chance you did the best you could. So be extraordinarily gentle with yourself as you fall asleep; you want to be rested and ready for the new day ahead.

March 2

Every once and a while, we're bound to have a day that feels like a near disaster. Looking back these will be remembered as "just one of those days" but in the moment, they can be very discouraging. All the judgments we make add up and weigh us down! Holding on to them consumes so much energy. One by one let the judgments go with a laugh and begin using all that energy to make the people around you feel good, valued and loved instead! Trust that things will work out just fine and then rest easy tonight.

March 3

Are you worried about tomorrow? Or are you finally learning that worry is the most over-rated, unproductive pastime ever invented? If there's some small step you can take tonight that will improve the odds for tomorrow, take it. And if not, (or after that small step) go for a walk or listen to some music, call a friend, see a funny movie, and go to sleep counting your blessings instead!

March 4

Our growth and change is often stressful to those around us. Don't let the resistance or lack of encouragement from others slow you down. Instead gently smile knowing that the pushback is very often a confirmation that you are making things happen and that you're on the right track.

"To be beautiful means to be yourself. You don't need to be accepted by others. You need to accept yourself." ~Thich Nhat Hanh.

March 5

Have you noticed that the days are getting longer? Suddenly one evening you notice that it's light a little bit later and that can only mean one thing. Small steps work exactly the same. You don't always see the progress day-to-day, but suddenly you realize that things are getting better, your life is moving in the direction of your dreams and spring is just around the corner. Decide what thoughts you want to take to with you into sleep and spend your last few minutes of the day with those thoughts on your mind.

March 6

If it's not your painting, step away and paint your own masterpiece! Sometimes we choose to move through our days without really declaring (and owning) our passions, purpose, and our right and to be happy and fulfilled. It seems easier to stay put emotionally, creatively and productively, and wonder "what if?" But when all is said and done, our lives are up to us and it's so much more fun to co-create with the Universe and see what we can make happen. Tonight get some good rest so you'll be ready.

March 7

There are lots of things that don't go our way but we still need to keep going. When we move forward with a smile and a sense of hopefulness, we are more likely to feel better and meet others who will inspire and motivate us to make important and good things happen. One deep and slow breath will begin to settle you down for the night - two or three, even better.

March 8

It's amazing what you can learn when you spend some quiet time alone. And it's astonishing and profoundly sad what you'll miss when you don't. Almost every answer you need is already deep within, and you owe it to yourself, your loved ones, and the world to discover them without further delay. If you feel you're ending your day with a list of complaints, think of something positive to focus on instead. Make a game of it and soon you'll be attracting more positivity into your life, which will give you even less to complain about!

March 9

Your potential is bursting at the seams and the call to action is undeniable. You recognize deep within that you have passions that are ready to be revealed. It's time to finally trust your heart, follow your intuition seize your potential and begin. Try going to sleep tonight with a smile; can you think of anything in your life to smile about? Look for little things and keep looking until you find something! As you smile, give yourself permission to relax into and shift into a "smile state of mind." Rest easy tonight, tomorrow is your day - you are amazing.

March 10

The goal is not to avoid the fears associated with an adventurous life. The goal is to be so busy living a good one, you hardly notice them. So, please don't feel surprised or guilty because you need rest, quiet time, alone time, meditative "be still" time. Saying "yes" to those essentials are just as important as making things happen. Quiet your mind; open your heart and sleep tight.

March 11

If you think good vibes are nonsense or over-rated, try smiling at a stranger. Actually, charity doesn't always begin at home. More often it starts someplace else and finds its way back home all by itself! You will attract people who believe in you and your dreams simply by believing in the dreams of people around you. Who knew it could be that easy?

March 12

There are times for each of us when we simply have to begin again! We've all been there and there's a very good chance we'll each be there again. And although the circumstances vary widely, we know that the solution is always the same: Begin. You (and all the things in your life) are perfectly imperfect. So don't wait until the stars are perfectly aligned to take a small step towards your dream. There is no day like today and no time like right now! You could go to bed without taking a small step towards a dream or you could figure out one very small doable step right now and take it. And then go to bed with a sense of accomplishment.

March 13

Why on earth would you choose to stand on the sideline watching the parade pass you by when you could be playing a trombone or twirling a baton? When you know what's been holding you back today, you'll know exactly where to look for that small step to take tomorrow! If we're getting ready for a road trip from snowy New Hampshire to Sunny California, it's okay to daydream about the sunshine ahead. But once the trip begins, our focus and attention must be on the stretch of road we're traveling on right now. The daydream is what gets us motivated and the car packed, the focus on the "right now" is what gets us to the beach!!

March 14

We never really get over devastating loss. In the thick of it, we almost stop breathing; sometimes even wishing we could. And we know deep within that we will never be the same. Yet, one day we feel the sun on our face again. We find ourselves smiling at a child or a joke or a memory. And at that moment, we realize we are finding our way back. Changed forever? Yes. But also softer, deeper, more vulnerable and more loving too. And we are breathing again. Sending a simple prayer that your rest is peaceful.

March 15

Some walks we must take by ourselves, not because we don't love or need others but because we also need to know and love ourselves. We're vulnerable and even needy sometimes. But even then we each have the capacity and power to get outside of ourselves and comfort and encourage others. Tomorrow, keep your eyes open for a "helping" opportunity and create a day that makes you and others feel good too.

March 16

Want to practice something that will change your life immediately? Practice looking at people with your heart not your head. Ask yourself, "What does my unjudging heart see when I look at Sam or Mary or that older lady in the elevator or that young man skateboarding on the sidewalk?" And then, listen as your heart opens. When you use what power you have for the sake of goodness, it expands. This is something beautiful underway in your life. Nourish it!

March 17

Happy St. Patrick's Day!

Your real beauty and your real purpose have very little to do with being perfect and wonderful for everyone else, and everything to do with being wonderfully real as yourself. Have you noticed that the people who put love, sweat and tears into making their dreams come true seem to be luckier? It's easy to be brave when everything is going smoothly. But when we're brave thru the more challenging times, we really get to know and trust ourselves in a deeper way and through that we grow and evolve into more grounded, wiser and more loving people.

March 18

There are three things I want you to know tonight:

Know you've done your best. You may want do better tomorrow but for tonight, let go of any self-recriminations and rest.

Know that your dreams are important and reflect your purpose and your calling. You may want to take deliberate steps towards them tomorrow but for tonight, let go of planning and rest.

Finally know that you are on the right path and there are many reasons to be hopeful. You can pick up where you left off tomorrow but for tonight push your worries aside and just rest.

March 19

When you are feeling fearful, tense, worried or stuck, just remember you've been here before and you've always worked your way through it. As you recall your personal setbacks and disappointments be gentle with yourself. You did the best you could then, and thru these experiences you've been learning, growing and getting better. You are so much stronger and so much more capable than you think. If you don't believe me, just look at all you've already dealt with and remind yourself – you are here on purpose! Tomorrow is a new day and there will be plenty of opportunities to begin again. Right now, your best bet is to relax, trust and rest; tomorrow you get a new start!

March 20

Tonight, you can be certain that you are a miracle already underway. The "start" button has been pushed, and where you are headed and what you are becoming is undeniably more beautiful, more magnificent and more important than anything you could imagine. And just in case you're not feeling it quite yet, don't be distracted. Instead, take another small step in the direction you sense is waiting. The feelings will catch up soon enough. Your capacity to love and heal lives, including you own is way beyond anything you could imagine. Way beyond.

March 21

This could be the night that you decide your dreams count and you're ready to begin making them happen. And if you decide that tonight is that night, it will become one of those pivotal, magical and beautifully stunning turning points you'll remember with a grin for the rest of your life. When you feel yourself tensing up, pulling back and feeling scared; remember you have gifts to be shared and whisper, "Yes." Then breathe, smile and whisper "Yes" again. Repeat until you feel the pit in your stomach releasing the tension. And then fall asleep feeling lighter and with a gentle smile.

March 22

There are things that you already know that you haven't yet allowed yourself to fully see. Many of us are learning how to speak up and speak clearly about what we need and what's important to us. When we do, we are often surprised to discover that people actually do hear us and respond appropriately. And if they don't, at least we've done our best to communicate and we can feel better about doing what's right for our own emotional well-being. And even more important, we can be certain the Universe heard every single word.

March 23

Often, when we make a decision, step into the unknown and dare to let go of the past to take a chance on our dreams, we feel vulnerable, unsure of ourselves, lonely and even scared. And we wonder if we've made a mistake or should turn back. These are the feelings that come with every great adventure so stay strong. Excitement, joy, feelings of soaring and self-confidence are just around the corner. If you take one small step towards resolving a challenge or achieving a goal today, you'll be that much further along when you get into bed tonight.

March 24

One of the most self-affirming and self-respectful things you can do is to stand up for yourself and what you believe in. In other words, be real with the people you care about. If, at the end of the day, that costs you a few friends, consider it spring cleaning and a life changing step to authenticity. Moving forward despite our fears and obstacles is one of the most empowering and powerful things we will ever do.

March 25

If you've reached a place where you're not feeling a lot of hope, take a small step towards a goal or solving a problem or challenge anyway. Once you do, you will begin to remember how powerful you really are and you'll begin to feel a little more hopeful. The more steps, the more power, and the more power, the easier the steps become. Soon you'll be feeling a lot more hopeful and that's when you know have turned another corner. Although I haven't walked in your shoes, you can be sure the leather on mine is thin in places too. There have been times for every single one of us when putting one foot in front of the other has taken every once of energy we could muster. Rest easy tonight, you deserve it.

March 26

Tonight, why not make life a little bit easier for others. Ask the Universe to put people in your path who need your kindness and attention. Trust me, you won't be disappointed, and there's a very good chance you will be amazed. Be the light for others that you are seeking for yourself.

March 27

Let's make tonight the beginning of a new era, where family is no longer just about flesh and blood but rather about hearts and minds. Let's no longer be divided by the superficial differences between us but rather let's be united by the deeper essence and beauty we share. Tonight I will let my guard down. I will breathe deeply and gently, and open my arms wide. I will trust that everything will be okay, and I will relax and open my heart to the goodness and light around me. This is how I will say "Yes" tonight.

March 28

The day comes when we decide that it no longer serves us to blame our parents, our family, our boss, our circumstances or anyone or anything else and we decide it's time to move forward simply because we're worth it. And that's the day, despite our circumstances, that we begin to discover just how powerful we really are. As night settles in, when you turn off the lights, use that "click" as a reminder that no matter how you're feeling physically, emotionally or spiritually right this minute, you have every right and every reason to be hopeful about more love, more peace and more opportunities to share who you are with the world.

March 29

You must know on some deep level that your mission is to touch hearts and lives in positive ways. Your purpose is and always has been love.

Tonight please remember to begin by loving yourself with all your beautiful imperfections and then grow by extending that same love, as best you can, to the people who appear on your path. Like many waves are destined to be one magnificent ocean, we are destined to be connected by one all-encompassing love. Tonight smile knowing you are not alone.

March 30

Tonight, be on the lookout for a sign. It may be a dream or you may notice something or see someone or hear a song, read a post, have an idea pop into your head or maybe just sense an inner shift. There are many kinds of signs but I have a very strong hunch that you will be reminded that things are changing; you are growing and hope is not just a nice thought, it's a reality that with each step forward makes more and more sense. Rest tonight so you will be ready to make a difference tomorrow.

March 31

Making some changes? Expect resistance: The bigger the changes, the greater the resistance. And don't be surprised if the resistance showing up is fear, procrastination, anger or confusion. Expect it because when you see it coming, it's less likely you'll fall for it! There will be another chance waiting for you tomorrow - an opportunity to do better, get it right, start again and or make up for lost time. Right now, the very best thing you can do to get ready for the new day is to rest without worry of concern. Simply trust that the "getting there" is already underway and won't be stopped.

April

April 1

First, you believe that it's possible and second, you understand that it's up to you to make it happen. Then you begin. Either we step up and declare that we are going to make our lives happen, or we sit back and watch life pass us by. Tonight dream about making things happen and tomorrow morning begin!

April 2

There are times when we have to ignore how we're feeling. Anxious, scared, unworthy, confused feelings must be set aside as we get out of bed and begin a new day. As we step into our lives and step up to the tasks that need our attention, these feelings dissipate and we discover that we are more powerful than our feelings, and that we have more strength than we thought. Dreaming without doing is like sailing while tied to the dock. Put up the sails and untie the rope and begin doing your dreaming!

April 3

Some of my favorite people have been discouraged and hurt. They have had their hearts broken and their hopes dashed. They have missed opportunities, had regrets and made mistakes. Their lives have not always been easy or perfect; they have endured sadness and worry, and have been confused and alone. And these very same people have gotten up each morning – the good days and the not so good days too, gotten dressed and asked themselves "Now what?" And the answer to that question has taken them to some beautiful, incredible and wonderful places. May you find a place of understanding tonight where you can accept that no matter what, everything will be okay.

April 4

Unexpected kindness given quietly to strangers who need a bit of hope is one of the most powerful forms of love there will ever be. If you can find real joy in little things, then you have begun to understand miracles. Love and positive energy are big and all-encompassing concepts. And just because we've never met in person doesn't mean that we don't care about each other. I am sending loving, encouraging, hopeful vibes out into the Universe as I write this; please let them in as you read this!

April 5

Many of us are reminded of those who have left the physical world and we miss them deeply and we feel a sense of loneliness and heartbreak. We sit quietly for a moment or two, closing our eyes and listening to the wind outside or maybe imagining the sound of gentle waves. And then beginning with a sweet memory and a smile of recollection, we open ourselves to receive some sort of other worldly but undeniable affirmation that we are not alone; we are loved and that our love will always extend way beyond this physical world now and forever and ever. Even when we feel all alone we are surrounded by light. Amen.

April 6

You can be certain that not everyone will like the short story you wrote, the cake you baked, the painting you painted, the way you dress, your hairstyle, or the choices you make. But you can be equally certain that most of these very same people would give anything to have your passion; and if they were honest with themselves, they'd admit they'd like to be engaged and making life happen just like you! If you're taking risks, pursuing your dreams, stepping outside your comfort zone and working thru fear and someone asks: "Are you out of your mind?" Take it as a compliment and answer: "No need to worry; I am working from my heart at the moment!"

April 7

When you begin to judge less and love more, you will have uncovered the biggest, most important lesson of all. Head into tomorrow cutting everyone a little slack, especially yourself.

You don't need to raise your hand and ask permission. It's your life and that's all the permission you need. When the inner you and the outer you join hands, you become the *only* you. And when that happens, things begin to unfold more easily and the trip becomes more exciting and fun too. Rest easy tonight!

April 8

The sound of sirens always gives me a pit in my stomach. Beginning now, I will use that trigger to remind me of the importance of community and how much I need and appreciate my brothers and sisters and their touch, their smiles and their love. Rest well and in gratitude, knowing you are not alone.

April 9

Every once in a while, it's important to do an overall inventory. Tonight find a quiet space to check-in with yourself; write down your short and long term goals, and articulate your passion and dreams. You'll then know what kind of a life you'd like (and deserve). And that's not only a beginning, it's a great one.

April 10

Think of the small steps you're taking as actual leaps that bridge the gap between where you are and where you want to be. You're not only making things happen, you may also be getting used to the thrill of being midair. If every time a ball player was up to bat, they hit a home run, we'd be bored to tears. Expect a few singles and even an occasional strike out. It all means you're in the game! If you are reading these words, then I am convinced that something good and significant is underway in your life. And by convinced, I mean *absolutely certain*.

April 11

It can be so easy to get caught up in the drama in the lives of others. The cure is to create a little excitement in our own lives. Every so often tomorrow, take a minute to hum a song and smile or laugh out loud. If someone should ask: "What are you so happy about?" Tell them, "I am brewing positivity, want to join me?" Waking up to sunshine is a decision, not a weather forecast.

April 12

Nothing is perfect. Not our days, not our friends or loved ones, not even us! How about simply owning this reality tonight Give everyone a little room to breathe and remember to take a deep breath yourself. There's something divinely healing about allowing ourselves, our lives and everyone around us to be real instead of perfect. And tonight that's going to be my mantra!

April 13

As another evening unfolds, let's pause for a moment and take in the rhythm and order of the Universe that surrounds us and includes us. It's so easy to be caught up in all that we need to do and all of our challenges, problems, goals, dreams, and worries that we forget that loving others and being open to being loved by others is our primary mission here. And as we remember this fundamental truth, we begin to realize that it makes sense to relax just a bit. It makes sense to take a deep, calming breath. And it makes sense to be hopeful because everything else will be okay too. Hoping you will rest gently and lovingly tonight.

April 14

Waiting for our lives to begin or restart or take off is a trick of the mind that keeps us stuck. Deciding that we're not going to wait another moment and taking one small step into the unknown is our soul declaring "I have begun." Starting now, I will focus less on what I want and more on what I have. I will focus less on my mistakes and setbacks and more on my potential. Finally, I will do my best to focus less on my thoughts and more on my heart. Consider this a virtual kiss on the forehead and a gentle wish goodnight.

April 15

Possibilities to give and receive love appear all around us. Be open and generous. When you share positive thoughts, hopeful words, and encouraging smiles you are held in the warmth and light that is created by your loving intentions and acts of kindness. Tomorrow we get to begin again. So tonight, let's seek and embrace a well-deserved and peaceful night's rest!

April 16

Honesty, a willingness to accept responsibility for my actions of the past and for my actions moving forward, a desire to forgive and an intention to trust, love and help others as much as possible are attributes of the people I want around me and the kind of person I am doing my very best to be. Most of us can easily identify our biggest, most painful mistakes. Most of us hold these memories close to our hearts, thinking that self-recrimination, deep regret and guilt is the price we must pay for the mistakes we have made. This is not true. In fact, these heart breaking memories are actually there to teach us how to lovingly forgive ourselves for falling short. They are a reminder that the only true way we will ever make amends is to learn from the past so that we can grow more deeply into our true nature by being more loving, kind and generous as the rest of our lives unfold. As we forgive ourselves, we are learning the art of forgiveness.

April 17

There are body slams, soul slams and heart slams, too. We can have the wind knocked out of us by unemployment, relationship transitions, financial pressures, and all sorts of unexpected, often terrifying scenarios. By now we have learned that life is not always gentle, or that moving on or even getting up and out of bed is not always easy. But we've also learned that when times are tough, we need to shift our focus to *action*. That's when we find one small thing we can do, and then do it. Then find another small thing and then another. It's the pathway to better times. You deserve to be loved and you begin by loving yourself.

April 18

I am convinced there's more than enough negativity in the world right now. So, I am going to do my best to be more positive about myself, those around me and life in general to tip the scale back towards positivity, love and hope. What you may not yet know is that you have a very important purpose here on earth and you have not yet accomplished all that you are called to do. Don't worry, your work is tied directly to your passions and will be fulfilling, meaningful and grounded in love. All you need to do right now is to stay open for signs that will point you in the right direction and also get a good night's sleep!

April 19

Who did you tell you loved today? (It's not too late!) Here's a little mantra you can whisper as you settle in for the night, "I will invite and seek out opportunities to lighten, brighten, encourage and affirm those around me. I will be open to receiving the light that is sent my way by those I know and those I have not yet met who are sending this very same light towards me." Repeat as needed. And rest easy tonight; you so deserve a little peace.

April 20

Tonight, imagine a warm, pure light surrounding you and keeping you safe and soothed. Rest gently knowing that as you sleep, your mind, heart and soul are conspiring to move you forward in beautiful and wondrous ways that will exceed anything you could possibly imagine. Welcome it in.

April 21

If you want to feel more hopeful and excited about what's ahead, your next small step could be the game changer. It's time for us to get serious about the passions we've been given. If they're buried deep, start digging. If we see them clearly, get moving. And if we're already moving, why not pick up the pace a bit! The truth is, being able to take that next small step is an incredible gift. Let's dream about it tonight and tomorrow morning, let's begin!

April 22

People who assume the worst, who find ways to discredit or bring others down, who instinctively discourage rather than encourage, who resent the success of friends and strangers and who gossip and share negativity every chance they get are typically people who have been deeply wounded. They have important and very personal work to do. In the meantime, do not let their toxicity bring you down or slow you down. You have important dreams to pursue and must always invite light and positive people to share the journey with you. Some very good people seem to practice worry until they discovered something better to practice: Gratitude and Hope. Have a grateful, hopeful and peaceful evening.

April 23

Don't ponder. Don't hesitate or worry about the outcome, what others will think or whether it makes sense. Just take a small step towards something important to you. Remember complaining, worrying and second guessing all use the very same energy that could be better spent, resting, doing and making things happen. Tomorrow will be another chance to use your energy efficiently, so sleep tight and get ready for a new day!

April 24

The simple, not always popular, truth is that you are responsible for your own life. What you do, and who you become is up to you. That's an awesome responsibility as well as an awesome gift – and it's all the more reason to make each day count. On some deep level we also understand that our purpose is mutual encouragement, healing, love and hope and that our light extends way beyond any earthly limits. Tonight let's remain open to and grateful for the blessings of our journey together.

April 25

What we say, think and feel is extremely important. But what we do matters more. Tomorrow you will have another chance to change the course of someone's day as well as your own, and with that the course of history. What an awesome responsibility and what an incredible gift! Rest gently tonight so you'll be ready for the new day ahead.

April 26

We are the champions. Finding our power when we're overwhelmed, confused or depressed requires us to do something even when we don't want to or don't feel we can. We have all been there, and taking action is the only way out. We may not be able to clean the entire house today, but we can clean out one kitchen drawer. Thinking is powerful, but to develop our intuition we must listen to a deeper inner voice - a voice that is part heart, part soul and part divine. And night time, when things have quieted down and we are getting ready to sleep is a wonderful time to listen.

April 27

Choose power over powerlessness. Even though we will probably never know the specific ripple effects of a kind word, a gentle touch, a smile, a handful of coins or a note of encouragement, we can be certain that our small and kind gestures are making the world kinder and sweeter. There's time enough for another small, thoughtful gesture and then settle into the night with a big smile and a full heart. It's good to want more love and peace in our lives and sharing it is the best way to find it. Sleep tight.

April 28

Sometimes that small step forward feels more like a stumble, but even a stumble is action, and action beats being stuck any day. Every storm cloud passes - Every single one. Living your life without hope is like forgetting the moon still shines when it's hidden behind a passing cloud. When you find yourself feeling troubled or anxious or overwhelmed or sad, think of something you're grateful for and say it out loud. Have a beautiful evening!

April 29

Sometimes we become stuck trying to figure out what's the right next step. The truth is we can't go wrong! So instead of trying to figure out the *right* step, just figure out *any* step. Take it and you'll no longer be stuck. During difficult days, sometimes all we can do is put one foot in front of the other. Expect the uphill climbs and then remember what's on the other side of every single mountain in the world. The good news is that one morning we'll wake up and realize how strong we really are, how far along we've traveled and how much better things have become! Welcome in peace tonight.

April 30

"If only . . ." is a time and energy drain. Instead, use that emotional energy to create possibilities and hope, and then make something good happen. Claim your birthright. You get to call the shots when you realize it's time for you to begin calling the shots. So simple it has to be true.

However smart or intuitive or competent or kind or as important or as powerful or as needed by this world as you think you are, you're not even close! Try multiplying it by a thousand. Okay, now you're getting a little closer! You were born of the light so shine! Let your light wash over others the way sunlight washes over the moon in the middle of the night.

May

May 1

If you are faced with illness, financial woes, unemployment, relationship or family stress, or other serious challenges that are weighing heavily, please reach out to others. I know you have been there for so many and the people who love you deserve the chance to be there for you now. Always remember that each and every one of us needs what each and every one of us has to offer: Love. Now is the time to ask, receive, offer and share. When you're willing to help, *and be helped*, you step into some amazing adventures!

May 2

Most of us wonder, worry and spend lots of emotional energy thinking about what's around the next corner. As you begin to re-channel even some of that energy into action steps leading towards your hopes and dreams, you'll not only stop spinning your wheels, but you'll also be co-creating what will be waiting for you when you get there. May the divine inner voice speak to our hearts while we are at rest tonight

May 3

Each belongs to those who claim it. That doesn't mean everything will go your way, but it does mean you are committed to taking at least one small step towards resolving a challenge or moving forward on a dream. You're pretty amazing because after all you've been through, you're still standing! With each small step forward through the difficult times, you're beginning to understand that you are stronger, more tenacious and more powerful than you ever thought. Tonight, as that undeniable truth sinks in, remember who you really are, and smile.

May 4

"Good evening" is much more than a pleasant greeting; it's a choice we get to make. What's one very small thing you could do tonight that would make you feel good about yourself? Make that number one on your "making it happen" list, because when you're feeling good about yourself, doors open, possibilities appear and you're much more likely to get a good night's sleep. During the daylight hours focus on making good things happen and then when you get into bed leave the rest up to the Universe.

May 5

Beyond a shadow of a doubt, you are here on purpose. Beyond a shadow of a doubt, you have gifts to share and lives to change. Beyond a shadow of a doubt, the best place to start is with one small step towards that place where your inner voice beckons. Just as steady drips will always fill a bucket; small steps will always change the course of our lives. We can't predict when the tipping points will come but we can trust that those breakthrough days will happen just as long as we do our part and keep taking those small steps. For now, imagine a peaceful blanket of warm moonlight gently surrounding you as you drift off to rest. Sleep tight!

May 6

Sometimes we stumble. Sometimes we can't see the light at the end of the tunnel. Sometimes we even feel like giving up. But, at the end of the day, we know that's just not who we are and we smile and know we will get thru this and that things will be okay. Rest deeply and awake lovingly.

May 7

You could decide right now to be open to an inspiration that will lead you to connect with another person in some small, simple and positive way that has the potential to transform a moment in both of your lives. If you are open and mindful, I promise the inspiration will come. And when it does, you will discover what a powerful force of good you really are.

The practice of worrying is a powerful and seductive habit. Many of us believe that worrying somehow protects us or is a price we must pay. These beliefs are simply not true. Worrying never really helps and always makes us feel anxious and powerless. Instead we need to give ourselves permission to think of or do something that makes us feel less anxious and even happier. Sure it takes practice but it's time now to begin practicing habits that bring light and lightness into our lives. Let's begin tonight - rest easy knowing that you and your dreams are so worth the effort. Tomorrow, wake up with the intention of honoring your dreams by taking a least one small step towards them.

May 8

We are not always guaranteed perfect or even easy days. In fact, some of the most optimistic people I know have dealt with some extraordinary challenges and endured many dark days. So, don't think easy days are always a good way to judge progress or success. Getting up and out the door on those difficult days and taking a step forward despite the challenges is a much more accurate barometer. There is something magical, miraculous and beautiful happening behind the scenes of your life. Maybe you can sense it but even if you can't you might want to begin to imagine it! Breathe slowly in and out several times until you begin to relax and feel more grounded. Sleep well; you've earned a good night's sleep.

May 9

You do not have to move mountains. Start with a small rock or two and repeat. Stay focused on the small stones and the mountain moving will take care of itself! Wishing you a sleep without worries and a new morning filled with hope.

May 10

On this Mother's Day many of you are remembering your mother with broken hearts, a deep sense of loss and an unforgettable everlasting love. And although you may not be able to send a card or have flowers delivered you can whisper her name right now as one way of saying "I will always love you Mom. Always." Thanks to mothers everywhere for giving up many hours of sleep they so desperately needed to care for and soothe worried, restless, sick, and sometimes just plain spoiled kids who needed and got a mother to love them unconditionally. And to those who are missing their mother today, always remember that just because someone has left their body does not mean they've left your life. Love is forever and ever and ever!

May 11

Tomorrow is another day - another beginning. Sometimes you're in the mood to begin and other days you have to take that small step even when you'd rather stay in bed. Either way, the day happens and there's a lot to be said for making the best of it! I am sprinkling a little hopeful, magical, love on you tonight and I am grateful to be on this journey with you!

May 12

As we take steps in new directions, we can expect all kinds of feelings that slow us down or even stop us in our tracks. One of those feelings is fear. A while ago, I discovered something very interesting about being afraid. Often what I thought was fear was actually, at least in part, excitement! And it's a lot more fun to be excited than it is to be afraid! The last things we think about and talk about before we fall asleep, stay with us as we sleep. So choose wisely dear friends.

May 13

If you took one very small step today towards something you've been dreaming about, and then followed that step each day this week with another . . . before you know it, you'd no longer be dreaming, you'd be doing! We each have so much potential to grow even deeper into the person we are meant to be. Tonight find a few minutes to be quietly alone and just breathe in hope and breathe out fear! And with each breath you will feel yourself going deeper and deeper and deeper.

May 14

If you're really ready to see how powerful you are, you need to stop thinking about all the things outside of your control and focus on all the things that are within your control. Practice using fear to your advantage. Dance with it. Don't let it paralyze you; let it motivate you instead. We all get scared – dancing helps. If we had a nickel for every time we said, "I can't," we'd have enough money to make any dream come true. So tonight as you fall asleep, be thinking "I can" thoughts.

May 15

You are the best thing that ever happened to you! Tonight, be the first to throw a small stone of kindness into your own pond and watch the ripples of love begin to change the world! Being real means being honest about how we are feeling. Don't discourage tears any more than you discourage laughter. There are times for each, and both are signs that healing is underway. Be real and sleep tight.

May 16

When we experience the kind of loss that leaves us broken hearted, lonely and somehow inconsolable, it's because the love and joy was and is just as powerful as our grief. So it's never really about pushing the sadness away; but it's about remembering and letting in the joy too. It's in those stunningly beautiful joyful moments that we catch a glimpse beyond the mystery and know in our hearts that love is not only stronger; it is forever. And we smile. Love transcends what we understand of time and space and is limitless and forever.

May 17

You couldn't eliminate risk even if you stayed in bed with the lights off and the covers over your head. Given that, doesn't it make sense to start tomorrow willing to take a chance on your own happiness? As we step into the unknown, we discover that we can be fragile, strong, terrified and brave all at the same time. Take that first small step tonight! More power to you!

May 18

Through challenging times you've learned how to pick yourself up, dust yourself off and begin again. And not only that, sometimes you actually make it look like dancing. You are, in a word, amazing! There are things that we already know that we haven't yet allowed ourselves to fully see. Maybe it's a change we need to make, a relationship that needs to shift, a goal we need to focus on, or a dream that needs to be put front and center. Simply asking yourself the question, "What do I know that I haven't let myself see?" is one good way to discover deep truths that can change your life in profound and wonderful ways.

May 19

From this day forward strive to be your own best friend. Look within for your dreams, your inspiration, and your sense of hope. Trust your intuition and your passion. Celebrate your strengths and be open to areas of potential growth. Believe in yourself, and remember that you not only deserve a fulfilled life, your purpose fulfilled is exactly what the world needs. And finally, never be too cautious to think big or too afraid to take small steps. Tonight invite in only those thoughts that calm and quiet the mind and then rest peacefully.

May 20

Things, especially life-changing important things, are often hard but seldom impossible! If you want the view, you need to climb the mountain! We each have our own challenges and difficult days. But even on our darkest days, our instinct is to feel grateful for the things that we do have and for the things that are going well. Since gratitude is the doorway to hope, once hopeful, we find the strength and the will to take one small step that will move us to better and easier times. It's the human spirit at its best. It's who we are. As the evening winds down, think of only peaceful things.

May 21

There is no one more important or less important than you. Your dreams count just as much anyone's. And the way to realize your dreams is the same way everyone realizes dreams: Action!

The first step is so important but it's only with the second step that we fully let go of where we were and that's when our next adventure officially begins. Sending you hope, courage and love tonight as you step into the beautiful space of becoming! Let the transition to sleep embrace you as your head hits the pillows tonight.

May 22

If you haven't been rejected, you haven't lived! We're all bound to get rejection letters, broken hearts and "no thanks" phone calls. There will always be someone who won't like our website, our book, our resume, our work, the way we dress, laugh, or tie our shoes (and they'll be happy to tell us, too). We've been taught that sticks and stones may break our bones, and words will never hurt us. But that's not true. Words are incredibly powerful, especially the words we use when talking to ourselves. Begin to carefully listen; what are you telling yourself about your dreams, your goals, your hopes and the challenges you face? As you listen, ask yourself if you need a re-write that is more positive, hopeful and encouraging.

May 23

When we decide to let our mistakes become lessons rather than regrets, we ascend into a more powerful and more logical place to view and live our lives. As we settle into bed waiting to fall asleep, there are often two tracks our mind can take. Tonight let's not get on the train that replays our worries, challenges, weaknesses or mistakes. Instead let's board the train that replays our blessings, our strengths and our dreams for the days ahead. If your mind gets off-track, bring it back to more positive thoughts and fall asleep inviting dreams of confidence and hope. You are here and that means it's a good night.

May 24

We all have experienced jabs and hurts and heart-break and betrayal. There is no way to sugarcoat those experiences and no need to either. During tough times we need to remember that things will get better and we look to the start of a new day to remind us just how resilient we really are. No one said getting there would happen overnight, but you *can* get there. No one said you were born with everything you'll need, but you do have what it takes. And no one ever said getting moving was easy, but a simple shift in perspective can change our moment, our day and our lives. Why not use this extraordinary power before you fall asleep tonight and see what happens!

May 25

People often point out that some "Begin with Yes" suggestions are easier said than done and speaking from personal experience I couldn't agree more. That said, there's a huge difference between difficult and impossible and easier is not usually part of making big dreams come true.

To practice forgiveness we must be willing to forgive ourselves. There is no one reading this that hasn't made a few major life mistakes; it's part of the human experience. Holding onto the pain and guilt is not only self-limiting and unnecessary; it prevents us from forgiving others. Tonight begin to let it go. Please.

May 26

How we're feeling isn't always a good way to judge what's actually underway. So many things, such as forgiving ourselves, being hopeful or being brave, are actually decisions we make and actions we take. The feeling part almost always follows the action, not the other way around! That's a very good reason to focus on the action today and trust that it will all come together a little bit further down the road! Tonight, find a quiet place to be alone for a few minutes and just practice breathing. With each breath, imagine your body relaxing and your heart opening. Trust that at this moment, you are here on purpose and things are unfolding the way they were meant to unfold. And as you get ready to sleep tonight, invite in thoughts of hope, enthusiasm and a vision for the days ahead. And rest easy; you deserve it.

May 27

Sure we're vulnerable and even needy sometimes. Resting deeply requires us to temporarily surrender the worries, the dreams, the fears, the plans and the circular thinking that tends to preoccupy our waking moments. And resting deeply is so important because it allows break-through shifts in perspective that will open new doorways that can change everything for the better. Now is the time for calm and peaceful thoughts. Everything else can wait.

May 28

An evening meditation could be as simple as quietly remembering
something good from your day or your life - even something as basic as
a smile from a stranger, a piece of fresh fruit or a soft pillow.
Remembering and feeling grateful is a wonderful way to end your day.
Grateful.

May 29

Self-responsibility, self-respect and self-esteem go hand in hand. Work
on any of these and you automatically see growth in all three. Instead of
taking your worries to bed with you, take your dreams. Instead of your
fears, take your hopes, and instead of re-playing your failures or
mistakes, remember the good people in your life by imaging their kind
faces, and then just smile yourself to sleep. The purpose of sleep is to
rest the mind and body. Tonight have the intention of doing both.

May 30

We are not just dreamers creating possibilities with our thoughts; we are
also doers, creating results with our actions! There is no need to
minimize your pain, confusion or fear. But remember that with each
small step towards the light, we are learning that we become more
powerful by exercising the power we already have. Dreams do come
true.

May 31

People who accept and celebrate themselves will do the same for you.
Those who don't, have some personal work to do and need some space

to grow. Tonight, why not give them the space they need and get back to making your dreams a reality. True love always starts from within and radiates out. When we begin by loving ourselves just the way we are, our hearts and arms open to accept, embrace and love those around us just as they are too. Whose smile makes you smile? Think of that person as you fall asleep.

June

June 1

How long should we wait for inspiration to strike? How long should we wait until we are certain we're making the right decision? How long should we wait until everything is perfectly aligned and success is guaranteed? The truth is we've already waited long enough. It doesn't so much matter where you've been, but where you're going. A little bit of trust and allowing things to unfold, combined with a little bit of muscle and making it happen will enhance the outcome tremendously. An authentic life requires action, courage, mistakes and risks because "the perfect time" is an illusion and waiting is a game we play because we're scared. Peace.

June 2

Sometimes our minds are filled with so many ideas that it's almost impossible to know where to begin. On those days we need to guard against overwhelming ourselves. It helps to keep a list of all your goals and challenges, and then add to the list as new ideas pop into your head. It's important to prioritize and focus on taking daily small steps on two or three of the most important ideas! Positive attitudes count, but if you really want to make something good happen, positive actions count more. You are here on this earth to do good and be kind. Sleep well.

June 3

Some days are just not going to be "surge forward days." There will be times when we feel like we're standing still and other days when we feel like we're moving backwards. The simple truth is that our vantage point isn't always high enough to really see or understand the big picture. On those days, take that small step anyway. The "adding up" comes later and you'll be glad today counted! It's essential to have people in our life to encourage and to remind us of our potential in a hopeful, optimistic and empowering way. We attract those people by being one of them. Give yourself a short pep talk and then get some sleep.

June 4

When we take small, consistent steps towards what "could be;" we are actually joining force with the Universe to co-create what "will be." If we aren't willing to look beyond our current situation, we will miss incredible opportunities to create new realities! Although it can sometimes be a challenge to do that, it doesn't mean we can't. Tonight, focus on the possibilities and get some good rest!

June 5

Sometimes fear holds us back in small ways, but other times it literally stands between us and the life we were meant to live. If you are not acting upon your heart's desire because you're afraid, the time has come to move forward. You do it one small step at a time, and you begin right now.

Regrets about past mistakes, wrong turns and bad choices are wasted energy. Of course, learn what you can, but then let it go. The truth is you don't have the perspective to judge mistakes and wrong turns and who knows? What appears to be a wrong choice today may in fact turn out to have been a very wise choice in a few days, months or years. The way to let go is to simply ask yourself, "What now?" Shift your energy from thinking to doing and get on with your life!

June 6

The desire to be actualized and working toward your full potential is an extraordinary gift and powerful guide. Your calling to a purposeful and meaningful life is clear but the destination and the path is only discoverable one step at a time. So today, we take another step.

Having an idea of what you want to see happen and then taking small, manageable steps in that direction is how lives change and dreams come true. And it doesn't matter how small the step is, all that matters is that you take one. Tonight why not think about what could be and tomorrow commit to one small step in that direction.

What your heart yearns for is not just a desire, it is a calling! Don't just listen, answer.

June 7

Make it your mission to find someone who has less than you and share a little of what you have.

It's kind of funny, we tend to think of small steps as really not all that effective, and we use that as an excuse to stand still. When in reality it's those small steps that make most of those big changes happen.

June 8

Let's expand our thinking about expressing love, choosing a more all-encompassing love that includes families and friends, people we work with or see at the store or gym. And while we're at it, let's include the people we pass on the street, buy our coffee from or share a short elevator ride with. And especially let's remember those in our lives who might appreciate (and even need) a smile and warm hello.

Later tonight as you get comfortable, head resting on pillows, lights out, (maybe the soothing smell of lavender close by) and with a stated intention of having a gentle, restful, restorative sleep . . . literally smile. Close your eyes and feel the smile from head to toe, and then begin to imagine a peaceful blanket of warm moonlight gently surrounding yourself as you drift off to rest. Sleep tight!

The real you is simply beautiful and all about love. Rest now.

June 9

Whenever we share positive thoughts with others, we just naturally increase our capacity to receive positive energy in return. It's simple, powerful and so easy to set in motion. Wishing you a peaceful, restful, positive night.

June 10

We are like a magnificent tree: expansive and deep. Our branches and leaves grow towards the light: evolving, reaching, unfolding and becoming. And our deep roots, ground us, holding us steady connecting us in solid, reliable and reassuring way. We may forget this but forgetting for a moment or two never changes who we are.

June 11

During difficult times, we still need to keep moving. We keep moving with a sense of hope and a little faith trusting that one day, one of those small steps will be revealed as one of our grandest leaps forward. You are much more incredible than you can imagine. But tonight, let your imagination run wild!

June 12

If you don't deliberately surround yourself with positivity, there's a good chance you'll be overwhelmed with negativity. Sometime we need a bridge and sometimes we are the bridge. No one I know has escaped troubled waters, rough seas and challenging, scary days. There are times in our lives when we could use a little help and other times when we are that help for someone else. It really doesn't matter where you are right now. What matters is that you remember we are stronger together and taking a hand is just as important as offering one. Seek out positive people, conversations, books and music and watch your spirits rise with your surroundings. And be that positive voice in the wilderness that others, like you are seeking. Lay down your troubles now.

June 13

At some point, you realize the sun was there all along - it isn't truly gone when clouds cover it, and it isn't truly gone when night falls. What your heart yearns for is not just a desire, it's a calling. It's up to you to listen and then follow. It's your pathway, plain and simple, and profoundly beautiful too. Tonight, as you sleep, may your divine inner voice speak gently and with great hope in ways that will stay with you in the days and weeks ahead.

June 14

There is absolutely no doubt that a positive, hopeful attitude combined with one step at a time actions create powerful new realities. And there's absolutely no doubt that you have what it takes to take at least one small step today. We can be scared and not brave but we can't be brave and not scared. So, don't be surprised if moving forward feels a little scary; it goes with the territory! As the evening unfolds, I hope you will choose to find a few minutes alone to think about all that has happened today. There is of course, great wisdom in learning lessons from our past experiences, but a much deeper wisdom in gently letting go of things that have bruised us and hanging on only to those things that have made us smile.

June 15

Smile a lot. When things are going great, it's easy to send out good energy to the people around us. But even when things are challenging and worrisome, we still have good energy to share. Of course, it may mean we have to dig a little deeper, but when it comes from a deeper place it's that much more powerful. Tonight, create a new, more positive and more hopeful conversation in your head and take a small step forward no matter how you're feeling or what you've told yourself. When you close your eyes to fall asleep, remember to put a smile on your beautiful face too.

June 16

Life can be hectic, confusing, painful and unpredictable and who knows what may be around the next corner. But we are learning that the human spirit prevails, hearts open and love surprises us, often when we least expect it. It's time to get over feeling guilty about taking care of ourselves. There is so much to do and there are so many challenges and opportunities to deal with, along with people demanding our time, energy and attention. Sometimes finding a little bit of quiet, alone time is the absolute essential "Yes." And in that space, we find our "Begin."

June 17

Tomorrow is Father's Day in the US. Father's Day can be a time of painful memories for some adult children whose fathers were not there or were there in hurtful and harmful ways. If this is your story, then also remember that you survived and your tenacious and hopeful spirit prevails despite the pain. There will be many wonderful celebrations and cookouts and family visits. There are many who will be missing their dads and instead of visits and phone calls, the day will be filled with memories and reminders of loss. If the tears need to flow a bit, maybe you will also find yourself smiling as you remember how blessed you were and that a love as deep as this never ever ends. When we finally and fully assume responsibility for our own well-being and happiness, we're assuming a very big responsibility. It's an incredibly powerful and beautiful opportunity too.

June 18

You deserve to have what is waiting patiently for you. But the ship doesn't come to you - it meets you halfway. A good life requires us to get in the rowboat, pick up the oars and put a little muscle behind our dreams. If you're on a journey that has you stepping outside of your comfort zone, don't let self-doubt throw you. Expect it to knock at the door from time to time, and be prepared to keep moving forward listening to an even deeper voice that says, "You can do this!" By the way, congratulations for moving out of your comfort zone! That happens to be where some pretty amazing things happen. Tonight, as you sleep, getting ready for a new day and a new beginning.

June 19

If I promised you a million-dollar reward for figuring out how to make your life more like the life you want, what would you do today to get a little bit closer? Of course, I can't promise you the million bucks, but I can promise a better life. And I trust that's motivation enough for you to get moving. Most people spend their lives waiting for "someone else to do it." Someone else will write that story, pick up the litter, stand up for someone being discriminated against, learn a new language or choreograph an original dance sequence. Every good idea, every problem and every dream that could come true is surrounded by people waiting for someone else to do it. Because everyone else is "waiting", you have the extraordinary opportunity and gift to step in and actually make something good happen! Every best-selling novel in the world began with one sentence. Every great painting began with a single brush stroke. Every person reading this has the power, the passion and the energy for one small step.

June 20

If you are doing work you love and are passionate about, you are blessed beyond words. Even if you aren't there yet, but are taking steps to move in that direction, you are also blessed. And if you are just on the verge of discovering you deserve to be happy in your work, you are on the verge of being blessed. Just because we *Begin with Yes* doesn't mean that we don't sometimes get discouraged and stuck. What it does mean is that we'll keep taking those small steps through those difficult times and that we' remember our track record which proves that despite our challenges, we not only can, but we absolutely will move forward. Sleep tight.

June 21

If we only could remember that we create many of our realities by how we react to things happening around us, we would begin to pick up our imaginary paint brush and dream up pathways that make our lives better! Excuses. We all have them. What are your favorites? Make a list and then transfer it to the back of a business card or small piece of paper to keep with you. Then every time you're tempted to use one to slow or prevent action, ask yourself, "Do I really need this excuse today?" Most times you'll be able to say "No" to your excuse and "Yes" to making something happen, one small step at a time. "I can do one small step at a time," said the person making impossible things happen!

June 22

If you want to learn to dance you have to expect a few missteps and sore feet before you're dancing with the stars. Honesty and direct communication is refreshing and sometime awkward. Provided your intention is clarity with kindness, it's always a more respectful way to communicate, leads to more positive outcomes and gives others permission to be honest with us too. How about a little emotional skinny-dipping? Let the world see the real you and you'll not only feel a new sense of honesty and freedom, you'll surge forward in unexpected ways too. When you are ready to share your gifts with others, you'll also be open to receive the gifts that others have to share with you. You are an incredible gift to the Universe so be seen and sleep tight.

June 23

When bad, tragic and heartbreaking things happen in the world, we often feel a sense of helplessness and hopelessness. Our sense of powerlessness overwhelms us and we feel like crying yet often the tears just don't flow. If there are actions that you are called to take, by all means take them. Then reach out to family, friends and strangers who are within reach, trusting that with each act of love, kindness and compassion our collective light will emanate far beyond our human reach in ways more powerful than any darkness and in ways that only God can fully understand. Breathe out worries and breathe in calm and then close your eyes and get a good night's sleep.

June 24

New realities are created by a clear vision, focus, hard work and a little faith. Identify a dream you've almost given up on and reactivate it today by taking small steps in that direction. If you go to bed with a simple doable plan for tomorrow, you're guaranteed to sleep better tonight. So, figure out one small step towards your dreams you'll take in the morning and then embrace the evening with a smile and a sense of hope. Not just sweet dreams tonight, exciting ones too.

June 25

From the right vantage point, beginnings and endings are really all part of a much bigger circle. So, resist the temptation to fear either and trust that one day your beautiful circle will all make sense. We are human beings. We take wrong turns, we make mistakes and we fall short. Through it all, we learn, we make amends and we grow. Then we simply must allow ourselves to move beyond our regrets and our disappointments into the warm light of self- forgiveness. Tonight, let go of any self- judgments or critical thoughts that keep you stuck in the past and sleep your way toward morning. Another chance to give it a go will be waiting for us tomorrow.

June 26

We've all had our share of disappointments, heartbreak, worries and confusion. And who hasn't screwed up a few times? If you're reading this, I am absolutely convinced that something much bigger, more important and much more beautiful than all of our mistakes and concerns combined is underway for you. Why else would you be here? I think you are way, way beyond amazing. Move into the warm light of forgiveness and sleep tight.

June 27

It is so easy to become overwhelmed and so unnecessary. Complicated and big endeavors need to be tackled and ultimately, be accomplished the same way long journeys are - one small step at a time. Oh, and one other thing: We need to begin. When you begin to judge yourself less and love yourself more, you will begin to judge others less and love them more, too! A powerful thought to take into this evening.

June 28

Our real purpose here is to love and be loved. Every choice we make gives us an opportunity to live purposeful lives and every step in that direction is a step towards the light. Storm clouds always pass. Always.

June 29

When it comes to your life, don't be a Monday morning quarterback. You simply don't have the capacity or the vantage point to evaluate what has already happened. Certainly, learn what you can from past efforts and mistakes, but then let them go. Save all that awesome energy for moving forward. You know so much more than you may think. You just need to find a quiet place so your heart can talk and your mind can listen! Have a beautiful evening.

June 30

"Yes" means having an open heart. It means being hopeful and excited about opportunities. It means choosing to believe that challenges can be handled and problems resolved. "Yes" means being willing to step into the mystery trusting that the path will be revealed. It means being responsible to change and grow and move forward one step at a time. And "Yes" means loving and respecting ourselves and those around us. "Yes" is a big and powerful word and the only way to express it and experience it all is to begin. The exchange of love is a force that is not defined or limited by miles, space or even death. It is powerful and healing and the most important energy that we can put out into the world. All it takes is intent, thought and sometimes action too and it is done.

July

July 1

Living your life without hope is like forgetting the moon still shines
when hidden by a passing cloud. The moon is still here, and so are you.
This is for anyone dealing with difficult challenges, loss, fear or
heartbreak. Most people know how you feel because they've been there
too – usually more than once. Since these challenges are never solved
with worry, let's for the moment put our worries aside and consider the
possibility that everything will eventually work out. Then go for a walk,
watch a funny movie, talk with positive friends, take a long bath, read a
good book, have a glass of wine or a cupcake or whatever is safe and
works for you. Banish every worrisome thought, at least for tonight, and
then rest that weary mind, body and soul. You so deserve it.

July 2

Broken hearts take time to heal. Most of us, if we've been lucky enough
to love someone who has moved on, know how lonely, painful and earth
shattering a broken heart can feel. I am not going to sugar coat things
because that wouldn't be fair or honest. But here are a few important
things that have helped me. Time helps, being honest with ourselves
helps, crying helps, letting ourselves feel but not dwelling on our pain
helps, talking about it with people who care about us helps, and
refocusing our energy on helping others helps too. It's also good to
remember that we will get thru this and there's an almost 100% chance
that this whole experience will expand our ability to take on a deeper,
even more meaningful relationship the next time around. For now, keep
breathing and make plans to make someone else's life a little easier in
the morning. I'd be willing to bet you've been doing the best you can. At
the same time, I'd also be willing to bet you're learning how to do better.
That's the point of getting older; it's our chance to also get better. Sleep
tight.

July 3

Want to help the people in your life heal, grow, feel happier and more content? Then pay attention to your own journey. Not only will you be paving the way for the people you love, you'll be showing them that it's not only okay to take care of yourself, it's essential. Life can be filled with so many distractions, but remember this simple truth: You are here to love, and the most powerful and transforming love is manifested when you begin by loving yourself. You may not be perfect but you are showing up and giving it your best shot. That's close enough to perfect for right now.

July 4

If you are working hard to keep everything the same, you're trying to hold back the tide with a small bucket. What outdated, limiting belief do you have about yourself that's slowing you down or holding you back? You can begin to let go by simply acting as if it's not true. Relax into change and you'll enjoy the ride and rest easier too. Walk on the wild side: Wear a wrinkled shirt, memorize a short poem or write yourself a love letter. Try a flavor of ice cream you've never had before, deliberately meet someone who seems different than you, smile at complete strangers, say yes to someone expecting a no, listen to a different radio station. Look for opportunities and then be open to exploring the unfamiliar. When you shake things up a little, your perceptions begin to shift and when that happens, you begin to see new possibilities. You'll realize that the planets are still spinning and the grass is still growing. If this can all happen without you weighing in, worrying or having elaborate action plans for tonight you can turn your problems over to the Universe too!

July 5

Life is complicated and filled with challenges that can stop us in our tracks and make us wonder if we will ever get to where we want to be. In these moments when our sense of hope is just a glimmer and we are feeling a bit lost or discouraged there's a wonderful question we can ask and here it is: NOW WHAT? When you ask this question and then listen, you will get an action idea. Then, no matter how you're feeling, take that next step. And then ask again. This asking, listening and taking doesn't always give us instant results but it does get us moving and when we're moving we do feel a bit, sometimes a lot better, and it also means we are on our way again! What you think or say may be important, but what you do is what makes things happen.

July 6

There are often people in our lives who discourage us from pursuing our dreams often because they have given up on theirs. Ironically, you may become a ray of hope for them by simply moving forward with yours. Let tonight be a time to recharge. As you fall asleep – imagine today's hurts and disappointments leaking out from the tips of your toes and evaporating. And then open your heart and welcome in the warm and comforting spirit of love and hope that have been patiently waiting.

July 7

Are you spending energy replaying and holding on to past mistakes, regrets or disappointments? It's safe now, and it is time to move on. If letting go is difficult, shift your focus to taking hold of something new. Taking hold of something new is often a small action step towards something hopeful and good! It's amazing what you can learn when you spend some quiet time alone with yourself. And it's astonishing and profoundly sad what you'll miss when you don't. Almost every answer you need is already deep within, and you owe it to yourself, your loved ones, and the world to discover them without further delay. You are here and therefore you are ready. Be gentle and forgiving with yourself and with others and rest easy tonight.

July 8

Most of us would love instant results. We'll lose 20 pounds in a week, write a book in a weekend, or get in shape by walking once around the block. When instant results don't happen, we lose interest or give up. Shift your focus to celebrating losing one pound, writing one paragraph or taking that first walk. With each small step the next one becomes easier and one day we discover that our clothes fit better, the first chapter is complete, and now we're jogging! And all began that one day. The light within may dim and flicker but it never burns out. Never. Let's fall asleep with a sense of calm and hope and wake up feeling excited and ready to begin.

July 9

Sometimes the events and life changes that threaten, confuse and worry us are life's corrections that will ultimately move us to calmer waters. This can be hard to believe when the sky looks so threatening and we are being tossed about by the winds and waves. But we are learning that after the storm passes, things are that much sweeter and surprisingly we find ourselves exactly where we needed and wanted to be. Sometimes taking an action step means taking a risk. It almost always feels safer to do nothing, so you need to decide if you want to feel safe or you want to make something happen. Hope is a powerful tool to have and a powerful gift to share.

July 10

Most of the time, we overreact to scary things. We lose our perspective and the level of fear we feel is not in keeping with the realities we face. Nevertheless, it can and often does stop us in our tracks. Tonight, remember that when we begin to take small steps we are no longer stuck in fear and we begin to regain our perspective. And as that happens, the fear dissipates and the next step is even easier. As you settle in, be gentle with yourself. Let the night be a soft blanket that invites you to rest. Remember your successes with a smile while letting your mistakes simply slip away.

July 11

Slowly, we begin to understand that pursuing our passion is not about our ego but about our purpose. And although there are many unique and individual paths, our shared purpose is always to bring more love, hope, compassion and light into the world. Let's focus less on what we want and more on what we have; less on our mistakes and setbacks and more on our potential. Finally, let's do our best to spend less time in our heads and more time in our hearts. Wishing you dreams that are love based, love filled and love shared. Sleep tight.

July 12

Feeling used never feels good. Standing up for yourself does. Being realistic doesn't mean that we have to keep both feet solidly on the ground at all times. Recently, someone sent me a thought provoking note wondering why I was so positive all the time, asking, "Is your head always in the clouds?" This was a new friend who had not yet spent enough time with me to understand that I totally get that life can be extraordinarily difficult. Most of us have had losses, heart break, physical challenges, illnesses, toxic relationships, major disappointments and personal challenges of every type and color. We really do get that everything is not perfect, easy or fun all the time. However, we are also tenacious, good people and we have hope, a little faith, a willingness to roll up our sleeves, and we keep taking those small steps even when we're scared, depressed or feeling powerless. Sure, we've had to dust ourselves off a few times but we're still here and doing our best. And isn't that something, all by itself, to feel positive about? Trust and Hope – Your key to tomorrow.

July 13

Some days, weeks, months and even years are easier than others. But most of us weren't born yesterday and we've learned an essential truth that makes the tough times a bit easier. We have discovered that we are stronger, more resilient and more capable than we use to imagine and more than that we know we will persevere and thrive again. Tonight, as you lie in bed ready to sleep, think of the people in your life that you care about and who have cared about you. One by one, whisper their names, picture them smiling and then offer them your blessings. It beats counting sheep, puts good energy out into the cosmos, and may very well have you drifting off with a smile on your face.

July 14

We are each a wave in a mighty ocean, and as our positive thoughts and actions join with our fellow waves, miracles begin, the world changes and our life begins to unfold with grace and passion. It's happening every day and that's all the proof we need. As you lay in bed, in that space between awake and asleep, put your worries aside for the night and with a smile, remember the people still here and those beyond who have loved and blessed you.

July 15

Sometimes we need to say yes to some quiet, think time. It can be as simple as walk in the woods, a long soak in the tub or a ride in the country. No matter how stressed or busy or overwhelmed we feel, we all need to create a physical and emotional quiet and calm space to reflect and recharge. The harder it is to carve out a time and place, the more important it is to do. And if it's seems impossible then it's absolutely essential. You don't need to pretend it's a priority, because it actually *is* one. Schedule it, commit to it and then make it happen. As you move towards sleep tonight, welcome yourself home with a smile and open arms.

July 16

What if you learned that hidden in every single mistake you've ever made was actually a specific lesson preparing you for the days ahead? That might shift your judgments about the past just a bit, eliminate any second guessing and make falling asleep tonight a little easier. Take a break from being perfect and enjoy being human. Because in that space, love, growth and hope are found! Fall asleep feeling hopeful about tomorrow; invite dreams of possibilities to visit while you rest.

July 17

Develop an imaginary but powerful invisible shield to protect you from people who keep you in your place, who discourage or drag you down in any way. Letting negative energy impact you is like deliberately banging your head against a wall. Enough is enough. Tonight remember your good, kind and loving qualities as you fall asleep. It gives them even more power when you wake tomorrow morning.

July 18

When you take one small step to create more meaning in your life, your life's purpose becomes clearer and the next step easier. Sooner or later you will need to begin. Why not sooner? We may not be perfect and we still make mistakes and sometimes we even get side-tracked. There are no guarantees but taking a chance improves your odds considerably. We are also moving forward, one step at a time and that beats giving up or staying stuck any day! Go gently.

July 19

You can experience gratitude, or you can *embrace* it by sharing your blessings. The first warms your heart and makes you feel good. The second warms your heart and changes the world. Is there someone you never got around to thanking? It's not too late.   Do something anonymous and kind for a complete stranger and your "thank you" will be received across time and space. Taking an action, no matter how small, sets things in motion, and that motion means that you are engaged with your life and making things happen. Wishing you restorative sleep and peaceful dreams.

July 20

We are here to make the world kinder and more meaningful. The passions we hold deep within are the key to doing just that. Always remember we are never called to sacrifice our passions, we are called to embrace them and then make those miracles happen. Become a lantern lighting the way for others and you'll find yourself surrounded by lanterns lighting the way for you.

July 21

It's up to you; no one else is going to make your life happen. If you're ready to own that, then you're ready for the next step. But being ready is just the beginning; you need to actually take the step to get things started. Remember, the step can be easy and small. Just take it and let the adventure begin. Sending love and peaceful vibes to each one of you as we transition to evening. Breathe in love and breathe out stress. Three deep breaths and you'll be ready to move towards sleep.

July 22

Yes, I can. Yes, I will. Yes, I did! Today counted! For some of us it was a good day and for others it was much more challenging. Either way, we are each here now for the same reason - to pause for a moment in the warm, supportive and caring energy that we are co-creating and so freely sharing. Because of each one of you my hope for tomorrow grows even stronger. Sleep tight!

July 23

Many of us are learning how to speak up and how to speak clearly. When we do, we are often surprised to discover that people actually do hear us and respond appropriately. If they don't, at least we've done our best to communicate, and we can move forward knowing a sincere and honest effort has been made. Consider talking out loud to yourself before going to bed tonight. Simply telling yourself to relax, calm or quiet down can create the shift you need to begin drifting into a peaceful sleep.

July 24

Life is not perfect, easy or predictable. Some days are simple and wonderful, while others seem like a runaway toboggan heading downhill fast. But no matter what realities we face right now, we've been given another day. We have more chutzpah than we think, and there's always at least one small action we can take to move us in the direction we need and want to go. Taking time to stop and smell the roses (or soak in the tub) is smart and much different than being stuck or immobilized because you are scared, depressed or confused. If you've stopped for the roses, linger and fully enjoy the moment. Often, during these wonderful pauses, the next step becomes clear! Tonight, imagine a warm, pure light surrounding you and keeping you safe and soothed. Rest gently knowing that as you sleep, your mind, heart and soul are conspiring to move you forward in beautiful and wondrous ways that will exceed anything you could possibly imagine.

July 25

Waiting "until" is a stall strategy that keeps you stuck, possibly bored, hopeless, unhappy and unmotivated. Shake it up and take a small step; when you're moving, you're not stuck. And when you're not stuck, you're making things happen. When things are happening you're not bored, hopeless, unhappy or unmotivated! We each, without exception, have an inner voice that is wise, hopeful and positive. Unfortunately, we don't always listen. And when we're not tuned in, we miss out on guidance, direction, and ultimately, on joy and clarity. A good time to practice listening is when you turn off your bedside light and move towards sleep. Tonight, rest easy and listen.

July 26

Sometimes we are like a flower unwilling to bloom. We hang on tightly to things that no longer serve us, and when we do, our hearts and hands aren't able to fully open to receive the gifts the Universe has planned for us. But when we allow ourselves to bloom, we not only receive those gifts - we actually discover we are surrounded by other beautiful flowers too! Tonight, remember that the human spirit prevails, hearts open and love surprises--often when we least expect it. The love that flows through us is unlimited.

July 27

Sometimes the person standing in our way is us. When we boldly take a step toward our dreams, we realize that the roadblock was only an illusion. And in that moment of awareness, the roadway opens up, our strengths appear and our sense of hope renews. As the night settles in around us, I wish you a deep and gentle sleep filled with dreams of encouragement and hope. As you rest, be reassured that the life you're creating is perfect, deeply good and filled with purpose and meaning. Only thoughts of love tonight!

July 28

There are moments and days and even longer stretches where things seem to come to a standstill. Naturally we feel discouraged, confused and stuck. But we are learning that taking that one small step, no matter how we're feeling, will put us on the path to better days. And so, even in those confusing and difficult times we smile to ourselves and decide that today, this very moment, we will begin again. If you know what you want, then you're one step closer to it. If you take a step in that direction, then you're actually making it happen. Think *small* steps and *big* dreams. Rest easy tonight; you deserve it.

July 29

Georgia O'Keeffe said, "I've been absolutely terrified every moment of my life - and I've never let it keep me from doing a single thing I wanted to do." It's okay to feel scared, but remember that fear is only a feeling. Then take a small step anyway. So many people have done it and are doing it - join them and keep your life moving forward. The truth is that most of us can't just stop worrying simply because it's a good idea. We have bills to pay, health issues that are scaring us, relationships that are failing and all kinds of real problems with no obvious solutions. So, to say, "don't worry" seems like a little too much to ask. However, let's agree to not worry tonight as we get ready to sleep. Put your worries aside for at least tonight. That's a beginning. Have a peaceful evening.

July 30

Reaching big goals, navigating major changes and making big dreams come true are usually not easy and most often are overwhelming. So, shift your focus and put your energy into doing one thing that moves you in the right direction. The payoff will come when you look back on last week, last month and soon the last three months and discover just how far you've come. Suddenly things don't seem so big or so overwhelming! Tonight, before you head to bed, think of who in your life could use a little encouragement. Who could use a note, a phone call, a cup of coffee or a flower for their desk? Then put that on your "to do" list for tomorrow morning, fluff up those pillows, and fall asleep with a plan and a smile.

July 31

Consider reframing dreams to get started. For example: If you want to be a Broadway actor, why not audition for a community theatre, or take acting lessons. It's a start and a hundred times better than doing nothing. If you always wanted to own a florist shop, start a meet-up group of people who share your love of flowers. Nurturing the essence of our dreams is always possible and that's where we begin.

As day transitions to night, recognize that things have also begun to transition for you in very powerful and very good ways too. And although it may be difficult to see, explain or even except just yet, let yourself feel a little hope and welcome and be open to growth and change and joy.

August

August 1

Sometimes our progress feels like a gentle breeze. We can't see it, but if we listen carefully with our hearts, we will hear soft, gentle music, like distant wind chimes beckoning us towards our dreams. We may not know what's around the next corner but we do know what makes us smile and that's where we need to put more of our energy. As you lay in bed ready to transition towards sleep, whisper to the Universe, "I am open to receive the guidance that waits." Then let yourself drift off to dreamland.

August 2

More often than not, inspiration strikes as you pick up the house, wash the dishes or fold the towels. You don't have to force it, just be open and relax into it! (And when it strikes, put down the towels and dance!) Night time can be a perfect time for reflection. Tonight, instead of reflecting on what did or did not happen today, imagine instead what *could* happen. Peace like a river.

August 3

As the evening unfolds, take a moment to remember the good things already in your life. Then with arms and heart open wide, gently move towards rest. As thoughts drift into your mind, carefully sort them. Those that are worthy and helpful will be used to shape your actions, and those that are unworthy and hurtful will be gently moved aside and forgotten.

August 4

I've told you that dreams come true when we take many small steps. Do you know that many of those steps take less than 5 minutes? If you don't have at least 5 minutes to spare for your dreams, it's time to reconsider your priorities. Right now. Make tomorrow the beginning you've been waiting for. Tonight, fall asleep with a smile, expecting that's exactly what's going to happen.

August 5

If you are faced with illness, financial woes, unemployment, relationship or family stress, or serious challenges that are weighing heavily, please reach out to others. I know you have been there for many others, and the people who love you deserve the chance to be there now for you. Always remember that each and every one of us needs what each and every one of us has to offer: Love. Now is the time to ask, receive, offer and share. If you knew how lovable you really are, you'd get in line to give yourself a hug! Rest easy tonight!

August 6

There's no finish without a start. At the end of the day, many things you thought were important won't matter at all. What will always be important and will always matter is whether or not you were kind and if you found the time to honor and pursue your life's purpose. Offering a glass of water to someone dying of thirst can save a life. A gentle word or touch offered to someone starving for a little love can, too. We're all in this together, so you are surrounded by light.

August 7

Don't discount positive thoughts, but put your energy into powerful actions! There are things that you already know yet haven't allowed yourself to fully see. Maybe it's a change you need to make, a relationship that needs to shift, a goal you need to focus on, or a dream that needs to be put front and center. Simply asking yourself the question, "What do I know that I haven't let myself see?" is the way to discover deep truths that can change your life in wonderful ways. And now rest.

August 8

If we're going to be discouraged every time things don't go according to plan, we might as well get in bed, pull the covers over our heads and turn out the lights. And that's just not how we roll. A deep sigh of frustration or weariness is actually restorative. When followed with a smile of gratitude, balance is regained.

August 9

Uphill climbs lead to spectacular views. Good nutritious stuff grows in the valleys. Be aware that each step you take is a new and unique part of your journey. Remember who you are and smile.

August 10

No matter how you're feeling - excited, discouraged, motivated or sluggish - you are so much further along than you think. You simply wouldn't be reading these words if you weren't. The day isn't over yet and there's still time to take a small step towards something that's deeply important to you. Why not right now? Rest your soul.

August 11

Begin to pay attention to how often you say no to yourself. No, I can't play the violin; No, I can't go to the party alone, No, I am not good at math, dancing, or meeting new people. Then begin to turn those around and say yes. For example, "Yes, I could play the violin if I rented an instrument, took lessons and practiced." Even a very small act of kindness (like sending a positive thought or prayer in someone's direction) lasts a very long time. Rest now – daybreak will be here soon enough, and we can take that next small step then.

August 12

There will be times when family and friends try to hold you back from your dreams and your destiny. It may be because they're afraid to move forward themselves, or they're afraid of your courage and successes, or maybe just afraid of being left behind. They have some work to do, but in the meantime, they may try to scare you, too. Don't let their fear stand in your way! Do you know who in your circle of family and friends supports and lifts you up, and do you know those who discourage and hold you back? Spend more time with the former. Knowing how important it is to offer words of encouragement and hope to family and friends, don't go to bed without picking up the phone, sending an email or leaving a note for someone on social media. The ripple effect of even the simplest act of thoughtfulness is often profound, sometimes even life-changing and always, always more powerful than you think.

August 13

We are no longer frightened children trying to find our way in the dark.
We are adventurous souls, creating magical paths, taking risks,
sometimes falling short, yet still bravely stepping into the unknown with
a sense of hope and purpose, surrounded by love and light. And that
explains the smiles on our faces as we fall asleep each night.

August 14

Obviously, we are called to love, help and encourage each other. But
one common mistake many of us make is trying to make someone else
(or everyone else) happy. It just can't be done. Instead we need to turn
our attention to our own goals and dreams - things that we feel passion
for - and by doing that we teach others, by example, how to seek
happiness for themselves. As you lay in bed ready to fall asleep
remember that those who have loved you and passed along are still with
you in many different ways. Be assured that their love for you is just as
strong and now even more powerful than ever. Take comfort in their
love and rest easy.

August 15

There is a natural cycle, an ebb and flow to our days and nights. As we
pay attention, not only do we begin to notice these shifts, we can
actually begin to take advantage of them. Some people refer to this as
going with the flow, and they are learning how to swim with the current
rather than against it. The best way to sense the flow is to take a deep
breath, relax and then listen with your heart!

August 16

Show me someone who doesn't have a dream, and I will show you someone who just needs to be reminded. Awaken to the truth that this is your life. Much of what happens is up to you. One small step towards your destiny is more powerful than you could ever imagine. We are a work in progress. Tonight, go to sleep with a smile knowing that you are growing in the right direction and that tomorrow you'll get another chance to begin again.

August 17

We almost never know when we are close to a breakthrough. So keep taking those small steps knowing that the next one just might be the one you'll always remember as that incredible turning point! Remember, we are one huge family, and you are surrounded by love, light and people who want your dreams to come true. Sleep tight.

August 18

There will always be people around who will be happy to tell you what's wrong with you, your life and the world. Look instead for the people who will tell you what's good and what's right. And, while you're looking, make sure you're doing your best to be that kind of person yourself. It's the "takes one to know one" principle at its best. We walk forward knowing there will be unexpected turns along the path. We step out in confidence because we know we can handle unexpected challenges, and we smile because we also know some wonderful, unexpected miracles are waiting for us too. Having hope when things aren't feeling very hopeful is the hallmark of a human spirit that will prevail. Dig deep if you have to, but hang in there and look forward with a little faith that easier times are ahead. For now, settle in for a good rest. Fall asleep thinking about the miracles to come.

August 19

It's okay to be discouraged, burnt out, exhausted, disappointed, heart-broken, afraid, lonely and immobilized. Everyone I know has been there. Chances are extremely good that you've earned that right the hard way. But the simple truth is this: The longer you stay there, the longer it will take to get to a better place. Rest well and invite hopeful, get-up-and-go thoughts into your dreams tonight as you get ready for a new day. Sleep tight!

August 20

Different thoughts and ideas resonate and make sense to different people on different days. Nothing, with one exception, could possibly apply to all people all the time. That one exception is the call to love more freely, with a sense of adventure and without expectations. It's easier than you think. Individually, we are many brush strokes, but together we are one beautiful masterpiece.

August 21

We not only need to sleep every night to rest our bodies, we also need to rest our minds. Many of us have a hard time turning off our minds. And when that happens, sleep is difficult and true rest almost impossible. Practice slowing down your mind by placing stressful thoughts on an imaginary leaf and imagine setting each leaf in a gentle stream and watching it slowly float away. Practice letting your worries out with a sigh and then breathing in faith, hope and self-confidence.

August 22

If you could see yourself from a higher vantage point, you'd be so calm and so excited at the same time. Calm, because you'd know that you are quite capable of navigating through whatever challenges you are facing, and excited because you'd see the incredible unfolding now underway. The beautiful flower is blooming and the beautiful flower is you. When our heads finally hit the pillows tonight, let's think about the people we love, those nearby, those far away and those who are sweet memories that will linger forever. Remembering each smile is a way to count your blessings and invites sleep to gently find you.

August 23

You can't begin to take hold of the new you without beginning to let go of the old you. We may have been ignoring it for so long that we think we've forgotten what we were meant to become. But on some deep and true level we actually know exactly what we are called to do, and eventually we begin moving in that direction. Tonight invite deeper dreams to visit while you sleep. And smile with sweet anticipation.

August 24

It's because of the mistakes, the missteps, the heartbreak, the regrets, the wrong turns and the lessons learned that you have become this somewhat weathered, extraordinarily beautiful being with a greater capacity for compassion, a deeper desire for authentic connection and a willingness to open your arms and your heart to express and receive the life force we've learned to call love. That's why I am pretty much in awe of you. When you are ready to own your uniqueness, your dreams and your potential, then you are finally ready to live the life that's been waiting for you to step up and claim it. Tonight let's remember that our very essence is peace, love and a spirit of joyfulness. As you remember, your world begins to soften. If everyone remembered the world would be transformed.

August 25

Want to practice something that will change your life immediately? Practice looking at people with your heart rather than your head. Ask yourself, "What does my heart see when I look at Sam or Margaret, or that elderly lady in the elevator, or that young man skateboarding on the sidewalk?" And then listen and watch your tendency to love more easily open a bit. Of course, there is almost no such thing as a perfect day or a perfect anything or anyone. Perfect only happens when we decide to view the world with a sense of hope, a little faith and a smile of self-acceptance.

August 26

No one is immune from storm clouds, dark or dreary days and difficulties that challenge us to the breaking point. But remember that it's always at that point that we discover three remarkable truths. We are much more resilient than we could have ever imagined; every storm passes; and the warm, bright sun does come out again. Tonight, I am here to remind you that you are a miracle already well underway. The start button has been pushed, and where you are headed and what you are becoming is undeniably more beautiful, more magnificent and more important than anything you could imagine. If you're not feeling it quite yet, don't be distracted. Instead take another small step in the direction you sense is waiting. The feelings will catch up soon enough. Some people look at a full moon and forget that just a short time ago it was just a sliver of hope! Sending hopeful thoughts your way tonight.

August 27

The secret to making something wonderful happen is to just go make something wonderful happen! Wishing for something to happen isn't nearly as effective or half as much fun as making it happen. Too tired, too old, too young, too depressed, too broke, too busy, too anxious? It's actually funny but most of us could easily claim being too something. We also get that these excuses are really just holding us back. Tonight before turning out the light and drifting off to sleep, why not do one very small thing that will move you closer to resolving a challenge or moving you closer to your dream. Once done, take a deep breath, pull up the blankets and rest peacefully. You deserve some good rest.

August 28

Tonight, reconsider the word impossible. When we clear our mind of all the meaningless clutter, we will hear life-enhancing messages from our hearts. The wind beneath our wings only works when we remember we have wings and we're willing to use them. Sometimes just gently gliding is the very best next step there is! For many of you, tonight would be a good night to glide.

August 29

There's no one who has dealt with the challenges you've faced, overcome the obstacles you've survived, learned the lessons you've learned and been given the opportunities that you now have. You have an important mission that includes goals to achieve and problems to solve. But you also have gifts, wisdom and compassion to share. The great thing about your mission and your sharing is that they go hand in hand. The timing couldn't be better. You are not just the little engine that could, you are the powerful locomotive that will! There is so much to do, so many challenges and opportunities to deal with and often so many people demanding our time, energy and attention. At some point we need to say, "Stop. We all need to have the space and time to settle into ourselves. When we do, we discover what's really important. When we don't, we tend to go in circles! Tonight settle in.

August 30

In this moment, we are each at different places and having different experiences. For some, it's a difficult phase and for others, things seem easier. Remarkably, despite our many differences, what we have in common is even more significant - we are part of a community. Although the tides will continue to ebb and flow, our love and hope for each other is clear and forever constant. There are endless moonbeams but only one moon. Individually our warm glow is comforting and sweet. Together our warm glow will light the night and change the world!

August 31

For what it's worth I do believe the good outweighs the evil. I do believe there are more people drawn to the light than there are those drawn to the darkness. And I do believe the day will come when love will prevail. Sometimes we need to say yes to more quiet time, to a good night's sleep, to a break from spending time with negative people, to more exercise (sometimes even to less exercise) and sometimes to some outside help. There's a very good chance you know exactly what you need to say Yes to. Since you know it, why not make it happen? Wishing you a restful, peaceful, hopeful night,

September

September 1

Even when we're feeling lonely, depressed, confused, without hope, angry or scared, we can dig deep and find the courage and strength to take one small step. I know because I have been there too. One small step is all it takes to begin moving us towards safer ground. Here, take my hand. We all deeply yearn for connection; that's how human beings are wired. And we can make that happen for ourselves and for those around us by simply reaching out a hand. So, across the Universe, consider these words the offering of my hand. I know that you offer yours in return and I know that you do that for so many others around you. Because of you, the world is changing. Thank you for what you are doing.

September 2

Things seem to be unraveling globally. There is no way you can listen to the news and not feel a pit in your belly and sense your heart breaking over the suffering being experience by people all over the world. Shock, fear, helplessness and despair are just a few words that come to mind. I will be honest; I don't have a clue how to fix any of this or even how to make myself or anyone else feel better. But I do know one thing. If there was ever a time when the world needed the light of good, kind, compassionate, and loving people, it's right this very moment. Those around you need your comforting touch, your kind smile of understanding, and your willingness to share what you have with those who have less. The world needs your compassion, your kindness and even your hope. Now is not the time to hold back. Tell the people you love that you love them and do whatever you can to make the world a little less hostile and a little kinder. It's not just the least we can do; it's probably all we can do. Your life is not just about accomplishments, it's also about contributing to the well-being of others. Once you understand and embrace that, you'll be surrounded by opportunities to move forward in both arenas, and the world will begin to feel better because it is better. You are not only surrounded by warm and comforting moonbeams, you are one.

September 3

Dreaming without doing is like sailing stilled tied to the dock. It's time to feel the wind against that beautiful face of yours! No matter how open your heart is, consider expanding it just a little bit more.

If you really understood how powerful and beautiful you really are, you'd be making even more good things happen in your life and you'd smiling a lot more at strangers too.

September 4

When you make someone else responsible for your happiness, sense of purpose and well-being, you are relinquishing your power and your responsibility to live your life fully engaged and full-throttle. This is not just your responsibility and your life, it's a gift more wonderful than you could possibly imagine.

Every single person reading these words is on a positive, life-enhancing path of self-awareness and self-actualization. And even if you don't feel it yet, there are absolutely no exceptions. So relax a bit and get the rest you need and so deserve.

September 5

If you're going to talk to yourself, be sure you're saying kind, encouraging and hopeful things. And then be sure to listen. Please don't feel surprised or guilty because you need rest, quiet time, alone time, meditative be still time. Saying yes to those essentials is just as important as taking all of those actions steps I'm always talking about! Sometimes even more important! Sleep tight.

September 6

Want to be a real gift to others? Nurture your gifts and pursue your dreams. Then you'll be creating something remarkable and authentic to share with the important people in your life! And after all, that's why you're here. Wishing on a star creates hope. Rolling up your sleeves creates results.

September 7

Life can be so difficult at times. We aren't expected to pretend that everything is all right, or that challenging, scary times don't exist. But we are encouraged to turn our attention away from those things outside of our control and focus on what is within our control. And when you come right down to it, it's not a difficult choice at all. It's not just okay to pay attention to your own needs; it is essential. An undernourished heart and soul has so much less to offer the rest of the world (including family, friends, co-workers and strangers, too) than hearts and souls that are filled. So please take care of yourself; the world needs you fully charged.

September 8

As you begin to trust yourself and your own intuition more and more, you will begin to move forward and make wonderful discoveries about who you really are. At the same time, you will begin to discern who around can be trusted and you will want to go deeper and build more meaningful relationships and friendship along your way. We can bounce back gracefully and easily or we can bounce back kicking and screaming all the way. But either way, as we practice bouncing, we'll become more resilient, stronger and more able to go with the flow in ways that will keep us moving forward despite the predictable obstacles and upsets that are just part of every life. Bounce easily tonight!

September 9

When we think about those big goals, it's easy to get overwhelmed and discouraged. Earning a degree, writing a novel, or losing 100 pounds are worthy ambitions, but they don't happen overnight. You begin by focusing on small steps to get moving or get unstuck. Then watch your life begin to happen. If you want to earn a degree, what's one step you can take to move in that direction? If you want to write a novel, what can you do that will set the process in motion? If you want to lose weight, what can you do that gets you a little bit closer to your goal? Big dreams come true when you take small steps.

Let's all just take a deep, deep breath together. Breathe out worry and stress and breathe in love and peace. Repeat as needed and sleep tight beautiful people.

September 10

We may not be able to predict the future, but if we actively engage with our lives, we can take part in its creation. If you knew how important it was to offer words of encouragement and hope to family and friends, you wouldn't go to bed without first picking up the phone, sending an email or leaving a note to someone social media. The ripple effect of even the simplest act of thoughtfulness is often profound, sometimes unexpectedly life-changing and always, always more powerful than you think. Tonight, as you quiet down and move towards sleep, listen to your heart songs.

September 11

Don't be afraid to be different, because that's who you are - different in the nicest, most wonderful sort of way possible. You are a tender touch, a helping hand and a gentle smile. And you are also much more powerful than you can imagine. One responsibility for those who have discovered their power is to stand up and speak up; demand opportunity, fair play and hope for all. It just goes with the territory.

September 12

Complaining is boring, wastes precious energy and keeps us stuck. Doing is exciting; energizing and makes things happen. And each moment of every day we get to choose which path to take. Settle into the evening and be gentle with yourself. Let the night sky be a soft blanket that invites you to rest and fall asleep remembering your successes with a smile and let your mistakes and disappointments slip away without a care. Now sleep tight.

September 13

Relationships of any kind are always a work in progress. They are not meant to be perfect, often bring up our deepest fears and wounds and often present challenges that bring us closer to a deeper understanding of ourselves. They are, however, meant to be loving and respectful. Think about the people you are in relationship with and decide how you might shift the energy towards growth and joy. Dream of the possibilities not the obstacles.

September 14

You have always been a beautiful, powerful, loving agent of change. It's when we forget who we are and where we're going that things becomes unclear. When we remember, the next step appears. Tonight, remember your innocence and beauty and desire to make life easier for those dealing with difficult times. You are not just moving closer and closer to the warm light of hope and peace, you are that light for so many others. Tonight, let's move towards rest with a grateful heart, not for all the things we have, but for all the potential we sense. A new day awaits your goodness!

September 15

Your intuition is your internal GPS. Some days are easier than others. Sometimes we miss a turn, but we always get to recalculate. Tonight, invite your inner GPS to get you ready for the day ahead and trust that there is light ahead and that arrival at your destination is assured. So, no matter how today went for you, give yourself a break, and rest gently.

September 16

You weren't given wings to fly, but you were given dreams to soar. Being afraid of an inner voice that tells us something we don't really want to hear or we are afraid to hear is human. Listening anyways is courageous. Some days we kick butt and other days we get our butts kicked. As the day draws to a close, it doesn't really matter if you were tossed about on the currents of the wind or if you were riding them. What does matter is that tomorrow will be here soon enough and right now you deserve some rest.

September 17

There's a fine line between helping and controlling. The people in your life will learn more from finding their own way than they will if being pulled in a cart by you. Show them how by example. Our own worries, fears and disappointments remind us to be compassionate with others, and our tenacity and resolve to move forward despite challenges reminds others that they can too. But right now, get some rest! You deserve it!

September 18

Self-respect and confidence grow with each small step that we take. However, life can be so hectic and the demands so many that we literally need to carve out time to sit quietly, as well as time to make something happen. If you don't schedule it, your time and energy will be depleted and you will always be on the short end of the proverbial stick. Schedule some time for you over the next few days and treat it like an appointment that's absolutely essential. It is! Let's all be done with ruminating and replaying worries, doubts and fears for the night and just rest peacefully.

September 19

Friends are one of the true blessings of life, but sometimes friendships require a friend*shift*! If some of your friends aren't encouraging you, believing in your right to have a dream and inspiring you to move forward one step at a time, then it may be time for a subtle shift towards the friends who are. Look for people around you who are helping others, taking risks, and acting as if their dreams matter. Tell them, "Thanks for inspiring me!" Now, give a deep sigh to release any tension and a gentle smile to invite pleasant dreams.

September 20

Don't worry so much about what if. Shift your focus to what now. Do you want to feel the effect of your power and influence? Do something nice for a stranger. When the inner you and the outer you embrace, you become real. And when that happens, life begins to make more sense and dreams begin to come true. BAM! Magic. Wishing you magical dreams tonight.

September 21

Tonight as you get comfortable, head resting on pillows, lights out, (maybe a soothing lavender scent nearby) and with a stated intention of having a gentle, restful, restorative sleep, literally just grin. Really, do it. Smile! Feel the smile from head to toe, and imagine a peaceful blanket of warm moonlight surrounding you as you drift off.

September 22

Some of us are facing difficult personal situations including: illnesses, surgeries, unemployment, confusion, depression and complicated or dysfunctional relationships. Be on the lookout for someone who could use a smile, a gentle touch or a few words of encouragement. As you reach out, your own life will change in beautiful ways. No matter what your circumstances are, you have the power to heal the hurts, lessen the pain and lighten the load for others. What could be more important? Your own tenacity is not only pretty amazing, it's pretty inspiring too! Rest easy tonight; you deserve it.

September 23

Most of us understand that although we can't always see it, the sun is always there. You will never have all the answers because each answer creates a new question. It's like dancing, and there's a sweet and gentle rhythm to it when you remember: One question, one answer. One step at a time is how life is meant to unfold. Now listen for the music and get some good sleep!

September 24

Walk a mile in your own shoes. When you do, you'll discover a brave and tenacious person who has gotten through so much, learned so much, and given so much. Be grateful for your journey and hopeful about what's around the next corner. You deserve that. If you don't feel a lot of hope tonight, take a deep breath and a small step towards a goal and or solving a problem or challenge. When you do, you will access your hidden power and you'll begin to feel a bit more optimistic. The more steps, the more power, the more power the easier the steps get. Soon you'll be feeling more hopeful and being stuck will be a distant memory.

Tomorrow awaits, but first it's time to rest your weary head and smile yourself to sleep.

September 25

What if, hidden in your biggest challenges were your greatest opportunities? You've been given a full box of crayons. But, if the beautiful picture you were born to create is going to happen, you have to actually open the box and begin to color. You have a choice. As you pull the covers up and settle in to sleep, you can recall and replay the things that went wrong today and focus on your regrets, your fears and your worries, or you can focus on the people and things in your life that make you feel grateful. Sounds like a pretty easy choice to me.

September 26

Think of your life as a beautiful brick walkway that you are building one single, solitary brick at a time. Sure, you've been scared, frustrated, angry and a million other things too, but have you ever completely given up? Nope, or you wouldn't be here. Good to know, huh? So, tonight, when you get into bed, just remember that the human spirit prevails, hearts open and love can surprise, often when we least expect it. Then, instead of counting sheep, count the bricks you've already put in place along your path and appreciate all that you've accomplished. Rest easy

September 27

Do not surrender your dreams! They represent your life's purpose and they need your attention. Instead, surrender your worries and fears; they've distracted you long enough. Being overwhelmed is a terrible feeling and a wonderful excuse. If we keep doing exactly what we've been doing, we'll keep getting exactly what we've been getting. And we all know what that means. You can lose the excuses and the feelings by taking just one small step forward. Count your blessings – name them one by one.

September 28

We each have our own challenges and difficult days. But even on our worst days, our instinct is to feel grateful for the things that we do have and for the things that are going well. Since gratitude is the doorway to hope, once hopeful, we find the strength and the will to take one small step that will move us to better, easier times. It's the human spirit at its best. It's who we are. Tonight as you fall asleep, remember you have been given an important life assignment. Even if you're not sure what it is yet, believing that it exists and trusting it will be uncovered soon is more than enough for right now. Sleep tight!

September 29

Some of us create with paint and brushes, some of us with words and some by raising loving children. Some of us create cakes that are masterpieces, gardens that are peaceful, while some of us can tune an engine so it hums like a choir. I only mention a few ideas to make a point. Trust me, you are a creator.

Every single event, mistake, wrong turn, disappointment, heartbreak and detour has prepared you for this moment. You are here to help transform the world into a kinder, gentler more inclusive place and you begin by reaching out with love to whoever crosses your path. Your tools are a smile, a touch, a word of encouragement, positive change in your own life, and listening. Before you fall asleep tonight, take a few minutes and think about the things that happened today that made you smile.

September 30

Feeling powerless and being powerless are two very different experiences. Although feelings can be very powerful, you are more powerful than they are. Practice being honest with yourself. Be honest about what you think, what you feel and what you want. You don't have to share it with others just yet, but you will experience an amazing sense of freedom and hope and begin to imagine what's possible when you begin to be real with yourself. As you move forward, be aware of how your hopeful, loving energy encourages those around you. You will discover that you are not alone and good people are being drawn near to love and encourage you too. Underneath anything else, you are a sweet, loving and lovable soul.

October

October 1

You have important dreams to pursue. If you keep waiting until the time is right, you'll keep missing opportunities to make something good happen right now. Big dreams almost always come true by small steps taken one day at a time. By taking just one small step towards them, you will attract the energy, encouragement and vision you need to take a few more steps tomorrow. Your heart's desire is not just about what you want and need, it's gets to the very core of your life's purpose. Tonight get some good rest so you can wake up tomorrow ready to pursue the dreams you've been given.

October 2

Peace.

October 3

We know life is complicated and we all have baggage. Some of us are packing a steamer trunk, while others travel lightly with a couple of t-shirts and clean underwear. When it comes to moving forward, we need to set aside our baggage and other distractions, and just for a moment focus on one very small step we could take, and then just take it. At the beginning of a new journey, all we need to do is imagine what's possible. Then take a bold step, smile and repeat. The faith and confidence will show up soon enough, but for right now settle in for a good night's sleep.

October 4

Sometimes it's the little things that we feel the most grateful for: a cup of coffee, a glimpse of sunshine on a cloudy day, an unexpected smile. When we remember that we can actually create these small moments for others, our power to do good is unleashed and the world is literally changed in an instant.

Sometimes a sigh let's out worry and tension and opens our heart for calm. And while we sleep, our dreams speak to our hearts about what's possible tomorrow.

October 5

Consider how your use words to describe what is happening around you. When I find myself complaining, I challenge the complaint, and more often than not, I discover a more positive way to frame it. When I do that, my reality shifts to a better more positive place too. Tonight pay a little less attention to what's happening around you and a little more to what's happening within you. You have an important mission here and if you quiet down just a bit and listen to your yearnings, hopes and dreams, you'll know what you need to do next. Smile, remembering what went well today and get some rest.

October 6

If we don't have people in our life who are cheering us on and supporting us during difficult times, we have some important work to do. Surprisingly, we don't need to look for people to help us, rather we need to look for people who need our help and then offer our hand. The rest will take care of itself.

Tonight be on the lookout for a sign. You may have a dream, or see something, hear a song, smell a scent, have a thought, or maybe sense an inner shift. There are many messengers and many touchstones around us. As we listen, we will be reminded that things are changing. We are growing. Invite in and send out thoughts of peace, hope and love tonight.

October 7

The only difference between an ending and a beginning is what we name it and how we decide to see and experience it. And of course, what we choose do next. You do know what's true. So listen carefully and act accordingly. Your dreams are a gift only you were given.

October 8

Make life a little bit easier for others. Ask the Universe to put people in your path who need your kindness and attention. Trust me, the Universe won't let you down and you won't be disappointed. In fact, there's a very good chance you will be amazed! Hope is not just a nice thought; it's a reality that becomes clearer with each small step forward we take.

October 9

Like a car parked in the yard, your life is not likely to go anywhere until you turn the key and give the pedal a little gas. Although the Universe might hold the car door open for you, the rest is up to you. If you are powerful enough to change someone's life with a smile, a touch or helping them take a small step, just imagine what you could do for your own life! Each of us has the power to follow our dreams.

October 10

Think of someone, not on your usual list of friends and family, and buy that person a cup of coffee or tea in the morning. Strangers count! I dare you! Light always triumphs over darkness, just as true love has no boundaries or limits. I invite you to whisper a name or two tonight, remembering someone who no longer has an earthly presence but who lives forever, surrounded by your love and light. Who did you tell you loved today? (It's not too late.) Smile, knowing love really is forever.

October 11

Sometimes all you can do is stand up and face the music. During those difficult, lonely or challenging times remember that songs come and go, and the next one will likely be more upbeat and easier to dance to. Dusk is such a beautiful transition time of the day. We are heading toward rest but there's still time to make the day count. In fact, if we took just one small step towards a personal goal today, we'd wake up tomorrow morning closer to our dream then we are right now. Hope you take that small step and go to bed with a smile. Fluff up those pillows and sleep tight tonight!

October 12

We have learned that life has its shares of ups and downs, good days and not so good days too. Sometimes life lifts us high with joy and gratitude and there are other times when we are frightened, heart-broken and just barely surviving. But we do survive. During the challenging days, we have every right to look forward to better days because we've been here long enough to know they will return. "Keep your chin up" can be an annoying cliché when spoken by someone who doesn't really understand, doesn't really have the time to listen, or doesn't know what else to say. However, when it comes from within, it can be a pretty powerful bit of encouragement that will keep you moving forward during those cloudy, challenging times. Plus, with your chin held high you have a better view of the opportunities ahead! When we look back, we recognize that we mostly did the best we could with what had. And when we look forward, we recognize we we've grown some and have more to work with now. We have a greater capacity to appreciate the challenges that others are facing and we simply understand how to make more good things happen. We are more open hearted with more self-confidence and self-awareness. And so we will continue doing the best we can, knowing that our best has gotten a bit better!

October 13

It may be all right and even necessary to spend much of your day doing the things you need to do to pay the bills, meet the expectations of others, and behave like a responsible adult. But isn't it equally important to honor the gifts you've been given and be grateful enough to find at least a few minutes each day to do something to nourish your heart and soul? You have a purpose and your passion points the way. Decide right now, before you go to bed that you're not going to settle for less than the passionate life you were meant to live. And once decided, relax and smile and get a good night's sleep!

October 14

Many people have a really difficult time being clear about what they want and need. When we withhold our truths, we prevent people from seeing us and interacting with us as we really are. Sometimes we do this thinking we're just being nice, but in reality, we're letting fear get in the way of authenticity. Not every day goes the way we want. Some days even take a turn that absolutely feels scary, overwhelming and beyond challenging. Don't let fear stand between the real you and your real life! Truth be told, there are no magic words or secret strategies that allow us to bounce back effortlessly or make everything instantly better. On those days be gentle with yourself. Remember we are human. Whatever the question, love in some form is the answer.

October 15

You really can't see a plant grow. The progress is so gradual that on a day-by-day basis growth is nearly impossible to see. But you can be certain that soon the day will come when there's no denying the bloom! You will very likely discover a certain magic as you begin paying attention to your passions and your life's mission. Also, you should be prepared for a certain undeniable power surge as you take a step towards a more hopeful, purposeful and meaningful life. You are stronger than you think and the life you want, deserve and were destined to live begins when you take responsibility for making it happen.

Tonight, fall asleep ready to receive guidance from the wisdom within.

October 16

If you're feeling lonely, visit an elderly neighbor who lives alone. When you're scared, help someone else be brave. When you're stuck, encourage a friend to take a small step. When you're depressed, make someone smile. When you're defeated, cheer someone else on. When your heart is broken, help someone mend theirs. And when things are going well and are unfolding the way you want, be grateful and bring someone else along with you. Tonight, before we fall asleep, let's pause for just a moment or two and co-create a collective thought that sends intentions of hope and healing to those in our path who may be struggling, overwhelmed, or discouraged. All you need to do is simply imagine a warm, glowing, comforting energy force emanating from you out into the Universe. I believe it will help and am certain it won't hurt!

October 17

There are so many legitimate things to be anxious and fearful about and fearful thoughts often spiral out of control. We also know fear escalates whenever we make it the focus of our attention and whenever we spend time with people who are feeling fearful too. The greatest antidote to fear is action. We take action not to ignore what's real, but to shift our attention from what we can't do to what we can do. When we do that, our fears begin to dissipate, we feel a bit better and we can help others feel better too. That's a good start. Let's make a few ripples tonight! I am almost certain that you know someone who could really use a phone call or note of encouragement tonight. It's not too late and you're not too tired. So go ahead and make someone's day a little sweeter. Sending you peaceful, loving and hopeful thoughts as you fall asleep tonight.

October 18

You, your goals and your very purpose here on earth is your call to action and nothing could be more important. The odds are in your favor. We may not always feel like it, or even feel up to it, but we still need to get out of bed and get on with our day. At least nine times out of ten, once we've started, things begin to improve. As tonight settles in, there's a gift waiting for us. When you turn off the bedroom light, use that clicking sound as a reminder that no matter how you're feeling physically, emotionally or spiritually right this minute, you have every right and every reason to be hopeful about a new day ahead where you'll have more love, more peace and more opportunities to share who you are with the world.

October 19

Without exception, we each have an inner voice that is wise, heartfelt and positive. Unfortunately, we are not always listening. and when we're not tuned in, we miss out on guidance, direction, and ultimately, joy and clarity. A good time to practice listening is when you turn off that bedside light and move towards sleep. Listen and rest easy.

October 20

Words can hurt. Choose carefully.

Words can heal. Choose lovingly.

Imagine the night sky as a warm, safe protective blanket that exists to comfort you and ease you into a restful state of mind. As you drift off to sleep, remember the moon is up above keeping watch so that you can put your dreams, schemes, worries and plans for tomorrow on hold just for a bit. Drift gently, remember you are safe, and rest well.

October 21

Want to get discouraged? Focus your thoughts, time, and energy on all the things outside of your control. Want to feel hopeful and make a difference? Turn your attention to all the things surrounding you that you can influence, change, and improve. For example, you have the power to change someone's entire day with a kind word, a smile or a gentle touch. You can help someone who is hungry or lonely or scared with very small deliberate actions. You can also absolutely change your own day and even your life by focusing on what you *can* do. And you can begin right now! Dream about that tonight.

October 22

Deep down you're a lover, and right now the world and those around you need your gentle, accepting and comforting embrace. One of the most wonderful and surprising realities we can discover is this: Whatever it is that we seek from others, we already have to share! If you can't be honest, clear and direct with others yet, at least be honest, clear and direct with yourself. It's a start. Often discovering and facing truths present our greatest challenges, but they also present the most incredible, game changing breakthroughs of our lives. You'll sleep better once you decide that yes, your dreams are worth it; yes, you're worth it; yes, you're ready to begin setting worthwhile things in motion. Now fluff up those pillows and smile because tomorrow's just around the corner!

October 23

When you look someone in the eyes and quietly say, "thank you" or "I love you" or "I could use some help" or "let me help you," and really mean it, you are making an incredible, life changing difference in both your lives. As lives change, the world changes too. Rest easy tonight; you deserve it.

October 24

Seek light in your thoughts, in the people you spend time and in your actions too. The transition to evening reminds us that life is about transitions too. When we understand that this is just part of the natural unfolding, we resist less and become less fearful. Everything will be okay! Rest easy knowing the moon patiently waits with you for a new day and a new beginning.

October 25

You may be gentle and loving and vulnerable but you're extraordinarily powerful too. What an incredible combination and what incredible opportunities wait to be set into motion tomorrow.

What I wouldn't give to just sit with you tonight and share tea and good conversation. And if we had that chance, here's what I would tell you: No matter how your day went, no matter what you accomplished or didn't make happen, no matter what you messed up or excelled at, *no matter what*, you are beautiful and well intentioned and doing the best you can. Best of all, tomorrow's another day and another chance! So pass me another biscotti, fluff up the pillows and sleep tight. You not only need it; you deserve it too.

October 26

It's amazing to discover that despite our delays, missteps and imperfections, we are, at this very moment, in the perfect place to take that next important step. We were not created to be perfect; we were created to be real. Real people make mistakes, take wrong turns and disappoint themselves and others even when they're doing the best they can. We were created to grow and learn and evolve. With that in mind, we need to be lovingly gentle and forgiving with ourselves whenever we reflect upon the past. Then we need to turn our attention and energy into using what we've learned as we love the people in our lives and embrace the opportunities and challenges ahead with hope. Dreams while we sleep are clues for when we're awake. Dream big and sweetly, you deserve good things ahead.

October 27

Purpose: always love. How we express it is the question. The answer is: multiple expressions, some at the same time, and many throughout a lifetime. Sometimes we don't realize we've been in purpose until we look back on it and then we see, "Oh, I was *in* purpose…" You have the power to change someone's life tonight – a call, an encouraging email, an idea, a contact, a positive post, even a smile. The funny thing is, when you do reach out, you'll discover that your own life changes too. Our capacity to love one another is limited only by our fear. Fortunately for us (and the world), we are not the kind of people to let a little fear stop us.

October 28

Putting a toe in the ocean will get you one step closer to riding a wave. Come on in the water is fine!

You have found your way here on purpose. You are tenacious and strong. You have gotten through difficult days and months and even years and you are as ready as ever to find a way to keep moving forward. Although we can't be promised only easy or perfect days ahead, we can be certain that we have important work to do, beautiful gifts to nurture and a purpose that is aligned with bringing more light to a world that desperately needs what we have to share. Tonight before falling asleep decide that tomorrow you will follow where your heart leads.

October 29

This may be a difficult truth to hear, but no one deserves to be in an abusive relationship or friendship. If steps to change it don't work, steps to move away from it are essential. And if you need help, getting help should be one of your first steps. Instead of figuring out who to blame, figure out how to make something good happen. No one is immune from storm clouds, dark or dreary days and difficulties that challenge us to the breaking point. But we can also remember that it's always at that point that we discover something remarkable. We are much more resilient than we could have ever imagined; every storm passes, and the warm, bright sun does come out again. It's impossible to love others fully and be loved back when we're not fully ourselves. Although this is how most people live their lives, we deserve and can have much more. When we become true to ourselves and begin sharing what's real with those around us, hearts begin to open. Rest easy.

October 30

Let this be the magical moment you finally stand up for yourself and your dreams and say loud and clear, "I count too!" You know many things. You are love and you are loved. You are compassionate and kind. There is deepness to you, deeper than you've ever gone but so familiar and good that just being reminded makes you smile. You are called to comfort others and will draw people to you who will comfort you. There is of course, much more but these are a few of the important things you must, on some level, already know. Tonight, choose peace.

October 31

It takes guts to be honest and speak clearly. You risk offending others; you risk getting a "no" or being rejected in some other way, and you risk being judged for being too direct. However, you also have the chance of being heard. We can learn important lessons from critical feedback, but the most important lesson we can learn is about focus. Learn what you can from the critical feedback and then return your focus to all that's good in your life. If you give people a chance to really know you and deepen your relationships, you avoid confusion, missed opportunities and the pain that comes with poor communications. So yes, being honest and speaking clearly is a risk, but when offered with love, kindness and comes from the heart, it's a risk so worth taking. Be peaceful tonight; be bold tomorrow.

November

November 1

Where we'll be tomorrow depends partly on what steps we took today.
Deep within each one of us is a specific life purpose. That truth can be
ignored, but it can't be denied. It can also be held at bay for a while, or
it can be welcomed in right now. The only one who can decide which to
do is you. That decision is yours - right now. Tonight, as you move
toward sleep, gently lay your ideas, worries, fears, plans, hopes and
thoughts about tomorrow on the bedside table. Then take a few deep
breaths. As you breathe out, let go of all thoughts of tomorrow. As you
breathe in, welcome a blanket of love and safety to surround you.
Gradually drift off to dreams, knowing that everything can wait until a
new beginning tomorrow.

November 2

We wake up and the day begins. We smile at ourselves and decide what
kind of a day it's going to be. As the day unfolds, we remind ourselves
what we are creating and find reasons to smile again. We can do the
same thing at night. Do you remember the last time you were content, at
peace, relaxed, safe and calm? Where were you? Can you remember the
smells, the colors, the sounds, who you were with and how you felt?
Paint that picture in your mind and then hang it on the wall near your
bed so the moonlight illuminates it, letting you fall asleep with a smile.
Those small steps can resume tomorrow.

November 3

We all have our wounds; some are hidden deeply and some are more
recent and clearly visible. But we are each in the process of healing too.
When we take steps to heal ourselves, we grow. When we help others
heal, we both grow. It's a beautiful thing and meant to be part of every

journey. Practice smiling at strangers, lovers and everyone in between. Your inner beauty will dazzle and change the world in remarkable ways. Fall asleep with a smile on your face - count your blessings not your worries.

November 4

In New England we're shifting from fall to winter. Many people have already begun to complain about the approaching snow and cold while others are looking forward to the seasonal shift and the changes that will bring. In New England, changing seasons are inevitable but fortunately our minds can create the realities that will become our experience of the winter months ahead. If you're feeling restless and don't know why, there's a very good chance that you're either avoiding something that needs attention or not pursuing a dream that cries out for a little loving. The solution in both instances is action. Just one small step will begin to curb the restlessness and actually move you along in amazing ways. There's still time today for a small one. Then settle in for a well-deserved, relaxing night. Sleep tight!

November 5

There is still time today to interact with someone in a way that shares light and love. Call it what you will, but practice sending positive thoughts, prayers, and good vibes unannounced to family, friends, co-workers, strangers in line at the grocery store or at the doctor's waiting room and anyone else you feel some intuitive call to connect with. The possibilities are endless and the goodness that will surround you will be experienced as a warm, golden light. Fall asleep with the intent to let your inner light shine tomorrow, even sweeter.

November 6

Tonight, before you get in bed, ask yourself what you did to move your dreams forward. There's still time to have a good answer. You already know what it takes to make something happen. The question is, will you take what you have and make it happen? If you have to lock yourself in the bathroom, take the dog for another walk, drive to the store for milk, or implement a hundred other possible strategies to be alone for a few minutes tonight, please do it! And when you do get time alone, ask yourself, "How am I feeling right now?" The answer is important and will guide you as you decide that next step.

Tonight, practice putting your worries on a leaf again, and one by one, watch them float away.

November 7

Stepping out into the unknown with butterflies in our bellies isn't all it's cracked up to be; it's a thousand times *better*! Some excuses are good and valid, while others are simply a game we're playing with ourselves. There are times when we can't even come up with a good excuse. In other words, we're stuck and motionless for no good reason. Good excuse, bad excuse or no excuse, take a chance and take a step. Move through those real and imaginary excuses and take back a little control over your life. One small step now is all it takes, and the journey ahead is going to be more incredible than any of us could even begin to imagine. Something wonderful and important has begun, and the mysterious and amazing next corner is waiting! A very good reason to smile yourself asleep.

November 8

We each have a very important life mission and we can be certain that it's tied to the passions that lie deep within. All we need to do is feed our passions by moving their way and trust that the practical aspects of our lives will gradually be revealed as the journey unfolds. Sometimes just gently drifting is the very best next step there is. Tonight would be a good night to simply drift gently into sleep.

November 9

There's nothing wrong with using training wheels; moving forward is moving forward. You're not required to have a positive attitude, a lot of energy, a plan for your life or even a clear picture of where you want to go. You only need a willingness to move forward. If you're ready but still feel a little unsteady, grab those training wheels and let's go! You are setting in motion something powerful and positive. Tonight be prepared for and hopeful about the positive ripples you are already creating and will create in the days ahead. Have a restful evening.

November 10

Getting up in the morning is good; showing up for the day is even better. We have not even begun to tap into our unique power to help heal the world and thus we have not come close to feeling the surge of power that comes back in return. As you move forward, be aware that your hopeful energy encourages those around you. You'll discover that you are not alone and good people will be drawn close to encourage, affirm and love you too. While you rest, give yourself a smile for making things happen, getting this far and for having a dream or two waiting to begin.

November 11

We not only need to sleep every night to rest our bodies, but we also need to rest our minds. Many of us have a hard time turning off our thoughts. When this happens, sleep is difficult and true rest almost impossible. Practice slowing down your mind by putting stressful thoughts on an imaginary leaf, then setting each leaf in a gentle stream and watching it float away. One by one by one by one... they go.

So many people choose to think about what's ahead with fear and anxiety. Another choice is to approach that next corner with a sense of hope and excitement. Practice the hope and excitement choice tonight and sleep tight.

November 12

If you truly want to celebrate diversity, you must begin by recognizing and sharing your own beautiful uniqueness with everyone, including your family, friends and co-workers. The world is so hungry for your authenticity, and the best gift you have to offer is you. We need you right now more than ever. Time to celebrate you! Tonight, pause long enough to be grateful for the person you are becoming - the loving, passionate, making-it-happen person you were always meant to be. Before you fall asleep, ask the universe to send you someone who needs your kindness and help. Wake up tomorrow prepared to be amazed and blessed.

November 13

There is a very simple way to find out what's going to happen next; be the one who makes it happen!

What are you holding onto that's holding you back? Sometimes it's a feeling or memory. It can also be an outdated belief about yourself or an unreasonable expectation. It can even be another person. All you have to do right now is name it. A small step perhaps, but so important that one day you may remember today as the day your life began to change. It's not just okay to pay attention to your own needs, it's essential. An undernourished heart and soul has so much less to offer the rest of the world than hearts and souls that are filled. Please take care of yourself; the rest of the world needs you fully charged.

November 14

We get up and get dressed. We brush our teeth, pour a cup of coffee or tea and we face the day, ready to do what needs to get done to make our lives work and honor our commitments. Then, because we believe in ourselves, and despite any excuses (many of them good ones), we do that little bit more to make our dreams come true. Since tomorrow is almost today do something today to make tomorrow better. Then rest, knowing you're already a step ahead.

November 15

Tonight, take a moment to quietly breathe in and appreciate that what's ahead will be perfectly enhanced by all that's been before. Our lives, right up to this very moment, have taught us, motivated us and prepared us for what is waiting. Tonight you know that you have good and beautiful things to share and the time to begin opening those wings has finally arrived. Rest now.

November 16

Being vulnerable, taking risks, allowing others to see and experience you as you really are, respectfully asking for what you want and being open to connecting in a deep and authentic way creates the opportunity for miracles to unfold. Tonight, before falling asleep, let's pause for just a moment or two and co-create a collective thought that sends intentions of hope and healing to those in our path who may be struggling, overwhelmed, or discouraged. All you need to do is simply imagine a warm, glowing, comforting energy force emanating from you out into the Universe. Just before you fall asleep, whisper, "Yes, we can."

November 17

Finding our passion or purpose isn't always a dramatic moment with fireworks and marching bands nor is it suddenly discovering a clear, very specific job that you are destined to do. It's not like you open a door marked "My Purpose" and suddenly everything is clear and your game plan mapped out. Most often it's a subtle, growing awareness of what makes you happy or excited and gets you thinking about and taking small steps in that direction. We need to take the pressure off ourselves to find the great big hidden secret and begin gently moving into the places we just naturally feel pulled and drawn to. Trying is the fuel behind every breakthrough and failing on occasion is actually proof that things are underway and success is on the way. Tonight, as you fall asleep, think about what things that make you happy.

November 18

When you begin to judge yourself less and love yourself more, you will also begin to judge others less and love them more. Just imagine what that could mean for you and the people around you too.

The last words we say and the last thoughts we think follow us into our sleep and visit with us much of the night. Being excited about your potential and grateful for your blessings is a good way to head into dreamland.

November 19

Sometimes we need help. For many of us the biggest and best small step we will ever take is to reach out and let someone help us. This journey is not about doing it alone; it's about figuring out what help and support we need to move forward and then seeking out that assistance. Taking that step is not a sign of weakness; it's a sign of self-respect, hope and strength. Just for tonight, take a break from all self-criticism. Remember that life is purposeful and evolving and you are growing and learning. Right now you have more inner resources than you did yesterday, and tomorrow you will have even more. When you let yourself be, you create an opening for personal growth. It's that simple, that important and that profound. Sleep tight!

November 20

Optimism is more about how we act than about how we feel. Most of us are ordinary people who go to bed just as weary as anyone else. We have the same challenges, make the same mistakes and have the same stress, anxiety and fears. But we are also extraordinary. We recognize that our dreams are important, know that our gifts are meant to be shared and believe, beyond any doubt, that our deepest purpose is to love each other the very best we can. That's why, when our weary heads hit the pillow, we smile. That's why we fall asleep with a sense of hope. That's why we whisper quiet words of gratitude for the day ahead and another chance to begin again.

November 21

It is essential to take your dreams seriously and nurture your gifts. The reason you've been given them is because you have something important and meaningful to share with the rest of us. You have what it takes, but you do need to take care of yourself in order to function at your best. You take care of yourself in many ways, including choosing who you spend time with, the books you read, music you listen to, what you eat and how much rest you get. The choices you make absolutely make all the difference. Choose wisely.

November 22

Thanksgiving isn't a day; it is a state of awareness. I am sending each one of you my love, admiration and deep gratitude for sharing this path with me. You are amazing, inspiring, very good people and I am so lucky to have each one of you in my life. Moving forward from today, let's remember that being grateful is a wonderful feeling, and when you turn the feeling into action, lives change. There's a powerful link between gratitude and sharing. When we feel blessed, we are inspired to make sure others feel that way too. Sharing actually becomes an expression of gratitude and that's the love that makes the world go 'round. Think of one blessing you haven't already remembered today and then fall asleep for a good night's rest.

November 23

There's still time to make today count. As difficult as it may be to believe, where you are right now is the perfect kicking off point for where you want to go. Take one small step in that direction and you will have the "begin" behind you. Isn't that a great way to settle in for the night?

November 24

Most of us are on a first name basis with Fear, but fortunately, our middle name just happens to be Courage. So, when we meet Fear on the path, we nod in recognition, but we don't engage. Instead we hold our heads high, eyes focused on the path ahead and we keep moving towards our dreams, one small step at a time. Many extraordinary actors I know have stage fright, but there's never been a successful performer who wasn't willing to push past the fear and step onto the stage. Engaged with their passion and their lives is where they belong and that's exactly where we belong too. Hold that thought in your heart as you sleep tonight.

November 25

The law of sharing: When you share goodness with others, the universe responds by gifting you with even more goodness to share. Pretty soon you are overflowing and the world around you is much warmer and brighter. It's not too late to make someone's day. The simplest acts of kindness create a ripple effect that keeps good energy moving and change the day. And when days change in positive ways, you'll discover positive shifts that will keep the road forward a bit easier and sweeter for you too.

Before you shut things down for the night, send a simple expression of love to someone you know who would appreciate being remembered. Then sleep tight.

November 26

Although we are here to make the world kinder and more meaningful, we are not called to sacrifice our light or our passions, but rather we are called to embrace them. The light we have to share is both a gift we've been given and a purpose we must honor. You have not even begun to tap into your own inner power. No matter how powerful you do or don't feel, dig down and discover a bottomless reservoir of guts, passion and hope. Open the door to your own capacity to take hold of your life and begin to make something happen. People just like you are doing it, and you can too. Sometimes all it takes is a minor change in scenery to shift your perspective to a more positive place. As today winds down rest easy and remember, when you wake up tomorrow morning you will have an incredible gift waiting for you - a brand new chance to begin again! May your mind quiet as you surrender to a good night's sleep.

November 27

Beginnings and transitions can be messy, muddy, confusing and scary. You may not have complete control over your days, but you have a lot more control than you think. Face each day with a smile, a sense of hope, an openness to the needs of others, and a willingness to step forward and move forward. Then you, and everyone around you, will fare better. Exercise the power that you do have and let the rest just be. Laughing helps and plenty of rest is essential. It's highly recommended that you get some of both.

November 28

During the holidays, many of us are reminded of cherished family and friends who have moved beyond our physical world. Although the holidays may bring moments of deep heart break and tears, stay open to beautiful moments of pure love and joy. Find a balance between getting things done and taking care of yourself. You have a lot to make happen. So, hit the pillow with a smile tonight, get the rest you need to face a new day tomorrow and please consider these words a goodnight hug.

We have no legitimate excuses not to listen to the song in our heart. And once we find it, there's absolutely no good reason not to share it with the world.

November 29

Living your life without hope is like forgetting the sun still shines on a cloudy day. Assuming there have been lessons learned, the only point in looking backwards is to see just how far you come. Sometimes that small step forward feels more like a stumble. But even a stumble is action, and action beats being stuck any day. The truth is almost every excuse has a work around. So if your favorite excuse is holding you back, don't delay. Create a workaround and make something happen. Acquiring things isn't what makes us happy; it's making things happen that does. What thought makes you smile and warms your heart? Think about that as you fall asleep.

November 30

The adventure starts to unfold when you say "Yes, I am ready to begin." What happens next is up to you. You can wait, or you can begin but either way, the next step is in your hands this very moment, this very night. Tonight as you fall asleep, imagine what could be.

December

December 1

In the hectic pace of the holidays ahead, some people will slip through the cracks. Keep your eyes open and be willing to slow down long enough to extend a hand when you see someone teetering. Know that you were there at that exact moment on purpose and that the love expressed in your action leads to profound inner peace beyond anything you could ever imagine. Within you is a light called hope; it may flicker, but never ever burns out.

December 2

We plant tulip bulbs in the fall expecting daffodils in the spring. That's exactly how small steps work and how dreams come true. Whether we greet the new day with hope and a Yes, or with defeat and a No doesn't alter the fact that the day will happen. However, an openness to embracing the day with a willingness to roll up our sleeves will make what happens better. By seeking out and surrounding yourself with positive and encouraging thoughts you are actually becoming more resilient, more focused and more opened to possibilities. You are connecting with others in loving, healing and inspiring ways. Although you may have moved forward one small step at a time you, have already covered many miles and the path ahead is now clearer and more open. Amazing, isn't it? Want to make the world a little sweeter and add a little sparkle? Then just let the world experience the real, honest to God, you. Sleep tight.

December 3

When you feel the need to begin letting go, shift the focus from letting go to taking some sort of action that advance a goal or dream. When we take hold of something more positive and productive, we are actually letting go of something (or someone) else less positive and productive. Small action steps count more than you can ever imagine. If you begin something tonight that you've been putting off, you'll be that much further along when you wake up tomorrow. Hallelujah.

December 4

Don't tell me how you're feeling; just tell what you're going to do. Actually, first tell me what you're going to do and then I'd love to hear how you're feeling too. Our days, our dreams and our lives have a way of slipping away from us when we are too passive, too timid or too patient to demand more. As of right now decide that those days are behind you for good. Lucky you, here comes tomorrow.

You are an amazing work in progress and worthy of a good night's sleep.

December 5

Tomorrow offers a new beginning. No matter how you are feeling, and no matter what your obstacles are, tomorrow you can stand up for yourself and your dreams and take that small step forward. And one small step forward is about as important as it gets. Often in our darkest moments we discover the strength to reach out and encourage, comfort and hold those around us. We are imperfect people but the call to love comes from deep within and that's what makes us beautiful and light filled even on our darkest days. Rest assured.

December 6

Tonight, remember your innocence and beauty and desire to make life easier for those dealing with difficult times. You are not just moving closer and closer to the warm light of hope and peace, you are that light for so many others. Practice shifting your energy, thoughts and focus away from what's not in your control and toward the things that are. In other words, stop worrying about all the power you don't have and get smart about all the power you do have. It's a game changer.

December 7

There will be times when people will try to hold you back from your dreams. It may be because they're afraid to move forward themselves, or because they're afraid of being left behind. Unfortunately, their fear can be contagious. The antidote is to spend more time with people who are moving past the fear and stepping into the possibilities ahead with a sense of hope and excitement. People with negative or positive energy have a force field that impacts everyone around them. It's the same with you. Deciding what force field to share with others and which force field to spend time with is a life altering choice we each need to make. Rest well and choose wisely. Just breathe.

December 8

One of the most difficult lessons to learn and one of the most powerful life changers you'll ever discover is this: the person standing between you and your dreams is you. Sure there are other people, circumstances, real challenges and problems to deal with, but until you realize that you hold the key, you'll be stuck and wishing rather than believing and moving. There is only one way to see what's on the other side of the door. The key is taking that next small step right now. Tonight as you transition to sleep, be more open to that inner voice and see what you discover, uncover or confirm.

December 9

Tomorrow there will be a stranger who really needs your smile. Perhaps it's someone on the street, in the elevator, in line at the store. You may never formally meet or even speak and there's no way of knowing for certain who that stranger is. So please take a chance and don't miss this opportunity. I promise your day will be better, and someone else's will change in a powerful and extraordinary way.

We can't predict the future, but we can choose to be hopeful. We can't control those around us, but we can choose to lovingly disengage from their dramas. And we can't prevent the busy, hectic holiday pace but we can choose calm moments. Tonight: Wishing and hoping. Tomorrow morning: Doing.

December 10

When we understand that pursuing our passions is less about ego and more about our life's purpose, we also understand that following our heart will bring more love, compassion, hope and light into the world. When we focus less on the presents and more on simply being present, beautiful shifts begin to happen for us and the people we love. You at your very core are one of the most lovable, beautiful, compassionate and brightest stars in the sky. It's time to let the world see you more fully.

December 11

Our individual actions can become part of a world-wide effort to make "peace on earth and goodwill toward all" a reality rather than just another holiday card slogan. It starts with a smile, a simple act of kindness and a little compassion. And it begins with you and with me, right here and right now. Amen.

Over the next few days, make an extra effort to be kind and appreciative of the people in the retail and hospitality business. These folks are working long hours, often for low wages, and dealing with way too many anxious, frustrated, stressed out customers. A warm smile, a sincere "thanks for your help" will be noticed and appreciated. Many of us have a list a mile long of things to do. We should know by now that we often set the bar so high for ourselves that getting it all done is nearly impossible. And when we do that we actually miss the moment because we are so focused on what's next. The only cure is to actually force yourself to take short breaks. Ten minutes resting in a quiet place, a cup of tea with a friend, or a short walk to get some fresh air will not cause your day to fall apart. It's guaranteed to help shift your perspective and make for a smoother, more meaningful days. There were miracles today. Did you see them?

December 12

As we begin to look back on another year edging nearer to a close, we realize that so many things can shift and change in a moment, a day and a year. We also know that some things remain constant, including our ability to live lives filled with compassion, kindness and love. Interestingly, comforting others is actually a great way to find comfort yourself. It's impossible to give a hug without getting one back. Your essence is love and nothing is more powerful.

December 13

The holidays are filled with so many expectations and we are tempted to put our energy into making a storybook happen for ourselves and people around us. This year let's not try so hard to make it happen, let's relax, open our hearts and arms and quietly see what happens. Sometimes, we feel called to support people far away who are dealing with some sort of catastrophic event. We can often help by sharing but other times, its love, not resources that's needed. In those instances, we can reach out and support those near us, knowing that our love and compassion will create beautiful ripples that in some mysterious and miraculous way will surely find their intended destination. I believe.

December 14

Deliberately looking someone in the eyes and directly telling someone you love them is powerful beyond imagination. It really doesn't matter what your beliefs are, what your religious traditions are, or whether you celebrate the holiday or not. The spirit of Christmas lives within each of us. And when we offer those around us a sense of peace, love, hope and compassion, we will truly and deeply experience the miracle of Christmas.

December 15

Giving gifts takes on a whole new meaning when you begin sharing the gifts you've been given. Share what makes you passionate and watch people around you come alive. The holidays can be extraordinarily lonely and challenging for many people. If things are difficult this year, turn your energy and focus to doing little things to help others. Even if things are looking good, turn your attention and focus to doing little things to help others. Together we can create miracles that will transform the moments ahead and the light in the forest and our hearts will brighten the world. Peace be with you.

December 16

It takes courage to be yourself and once you start down that path you won't want to turn back. Of course not everyone will understand, support of even like you. So what! At this time of year especially, we need to say *Yes* to some quiet, think-time. It can be as simple as a walk in the woods, a long soak in the bathtub, or a ride in the country. No matter how stressed or busy or overwhelmed we feel, we all need to create a physical and emotional quiet and calm space to reflect and recharge. The harder it is to carve out a time and place, the more important it is to do. If it seems impossible, then it's essential. Rest tonight and fall asleep intending to be gentle with yourself and those around you tomorrow.

December 17

A shout out to all the restaurant workers, wait staff, taxi drivers, baggage handlers and all the other people who make life easier for us not only during the holidays but all year long. Take a moment to say thanks and remember your tip for good service is a big part of their income, and a little extra heartfelt generosity during the holidays is always welcomed. When you smile, even when you don't feel like it, you are opening the pathway to your heart. Once the pathway is opened the next smile comes easier. That's why smiles are contagious and instantly connect people heart to heart. Be sure you're not focusing all your time and energy on all those things that don't really matter while forgetting or neglecting all those that really do. If you have family and friends dealing with heartbreak during the holiday season, remember when words fail, a gentle touch, a hug or a note of support can gently bring those we care about back to a place of light, hope and love. Before you go to sleep tonight identify one person who you will encourage tomorrow and decide how you'll do it. With that plan in place, rest easy knowing something good is just around the corner.

December 18

When it comes to who you really are, the colorful ribbon and beautiful paper on the outside is nothing compared to the incredibly beautiful person within. You are a precious gift. To all the good people in my life (many of whom are reading this now), who add joy, hope and inspiration to my world, I send you my gratitude and love, wishing you sweet dreams and a peaceful night.

December 19

No matter how busy we are, let's find a few minutes for some thoughtful, deliberate, loving energy directed towards someone in our life who may be struggling a bit with the holidays. Maybe it's a neighbor, a co-worker, a friend or even a stranger. Make things a little easier, sweeter and more peaceful for that person, and you'll discover the real purpose behind all the celebrations. The call to love is not about an individual relationship, it's about your relationship with the world. When you find yourself feeling troubled, anxious, overwhelmed or sad, think of something you're grateful for and say it out loud, or whisper it if you need to. Repeat as needed.

December 20

For those who aren't anticipating a storybook holiday this year - maybe you're grieving a loss, or are lonely, discouraged or worried about the challenges you face - you can be certain that everyone else has struggled through a holiday or two. Be gentle with yourself, stay open to the kindness of others and stay open to some small Christmas miracle too. Remember, story book stories are, after all, just stories.

Tonight you may be exhausted, worn out, and have a list of things to do tomorrow that's a mile long. Take a deep breath, sigh if that helps and then give yourself credit for making so much happen and getting so much done over the past few days. Right now, the word of the hour is *enough*. Sleep well.

December 21

You are not perfect and like all of us you have good moments and not so good moments too. But you do know how to love. For many, you are leading the way to a saner, calmer, more loving world. Remember that as tomorrow unfolds. This is a great time to remember and appreciate all the Direct Support Professionals and healthcare workers who are loving caregivers for our elderly parents, our loved ones with special needs and our brothers, sisters, and friends who need a little assistance to live meaningful lives. Whoever coined the phrase "angels walking among us" must have seen a care-giver in action and recognized how incredibly important and beautiful they are. I believe in angels.

December 22

To those missing love ones this Christmas, whether the loss is recent and your grief runs deep or it's been a very long time and what's left is a lingering sense of melancholy. Either way, there's an empty space in your heart that can't quite be filled no matter how long it's been, or how many other wonderful people are in your life to love and who are loving you back. As you remember, may you feel their eternal presence, with you and in your heart forever. Everyone has heard Christmas music and felt lonely and sad at one time or another. We don't need to discount our realities or our feelings but it does make sense to make room for other more hopeful feelings too. The best way to do that is to reach out, the best you can and make the holidays a little sweeter for someone else. We humans are like a string of Christmas lights, more beautiful because we stick together. Peace.

December 23

Tomorrow you will be given many small opportunities to change someone's moment, day or even life for the better. What if every night was a holy night? Peaceful and restorative, with beautiful dreams that nurtured our passions and encouraged and lifted us up. What if every night, before we fell asleep we whispered the truth, "Oh, Holy Night"? Blessings.

December 24

This is our one and only chance to experience today, so let's embrace it with love, hope, compassion and kindness. To each and all of the generous and loving people in my life, you will never know the ripple effect of your good and loving energy, which is the real meaning of Christmas and you are making such a beautiful difference. Of that you can be certain. Thanks for being here with me. I love you.

Rest now. The stars will keep watch.

December 25

If you take a single moment today to quietly remember your non-tangible blessings and gifts, your day will be so much sweeter and more meaningful. I hope you had a wonderful day! We are often disappointed that realities don't live up to our expectations. Fortunately, that doesn't stop those unexpected little miracles or heartwarming moments or memories that seem to appear out of nowhere. At the end of the day, as we wash the last few dishes and turn off the Christmas lights, alone with our thoughts at last, we realize that everything is okay. And in that moment, we blow out the last candle with a smile of gratitude for what's behind us and pull back the covers with a sense of hope for what's ahead. And we rest.

December 26

Some may think that the holiday is over, but the real celebration is just beginning. It begins fresh each day and never ends when we embrace joy, hope, kindness, and togetherness, not just for one special day, but from each day forward. The day after anything always represents a new beginning. There's a new feeling in the air and today it somehow feels like anything is possible. A good question to ask as another year begins to winds down is, "What have I learned the hard way, and what has it taught me to do differently?" Tonight as you get ready for bed, the answers will help you remember just how far you've come and what direction you need to head.

December 27

Some of us have a real struggle making decisions! We get so tangled weighing the pros and cons that we stay stuck. It's an unfortunate and unnecessary game we play with ourselves because truth be told, decisions are almost always based on an educated guess and the course can always be modified. Most of us wonder, worry and spend too much emotional energy thinking about what's around the next corner. As we begin to re-channel some of that "wondering/worrying" energy into action steps leading towards our hopes and dreams, we'll not only stop spinning our wheels, we'll be co-creating what will be waiting when we get there. Take a step even if you're confused - you are here with purpose. Passion and compassion are what you have to offer and they are exactly what the world needs most. Now get some rest and be ready to share tomorrow.

December 28

Flowers need the rain to grow. So do we. Create a mental delete button and practice deleting negative thoughts. When a self-defeating thought pops into your head, visualize that delete button, take your finger and press it firmly. Then replace that negative thought that was holding you back with a more positive, encouraging and hopeful one. Repeat as necessary. You still have more than a few doors to discover and open and a more than a few of your own gifts to embrace and share. As the New Year gets closer, so do your chances to make something good and important happen in your life. You can decide right now that you've waited long enough and trust that the year ahead will welcome you with open arms. Once you've made that decision, take a moment to let it sink in, take a deep breath and then get back to all the things demanding your attention today. In the very darkest moments our light may flicker but it does not go out. It never ever goes out.

December 29

We're getting closer to the beginning of the New Year, and if you're not already outside of your comfort zone, there's never been a better time.

Sure it can be scary, but it's also exciting. A little scared and a little excited is a great way to begin. Here we go! We never really know who we might meet. Since even our best friends were once strangers, it makes the new day ahead kind of exciting. If you wake up tomorrow willing to embrace the power of *Yes*, you'll wake up tomorrow ready to discover the power of *You*.

December 30

You truly inspire me every single day and I can't begin to imagine how many lives you've touched by your open, honest and kind spirit. I feel extraordinarily blessed to be on this path with you. Are you finally ready to accept your gifts and your passions as signs that it's time to listen to your heart? And as you listen, are you finally ready to step into your life in a deeper more action-oriented way? I hope so; the New Year is just ahead. Three things will last forever: faith, hope, and love. And the greatest of these is love!

December 31

Are you ready? Does a new beginning sound like a good plan? Are you ready to say *Yes* to your dreams, your goals, and your hopes? Are you ready to say *Yes* to solving your problems and facing your challenges? If you are, then you are about to begin your most incredible and revolutionary year yet. Sometimes we just know in our gut that it's time for that leap of faith. This year is just about over. Sure there have been successes and disappointments and plenty of ups and downs. We've made our share of mistakes, and not everything has worked out the way we thought or hoped it would. But guess what? We showed up. We're still here. We did our best and would have done better if we could have. So with no regrets and with a growing sense of hope, "Welcome the New Year!" (I am imagining fireworks.) See you in the New Year.

Other books by Paul Boynton

Begin with Yes
A short conversation that will change your life forever

Begin with Yes – 21 Day Companion Workbook
A step-by-step guide to living your Begin with Yes life

Begin with Yes – Action Planner
Chart your course. Track your progress. Make Dreams happen!

Beginnings – A Daily Guide for Adventurous Souls
Morning affirmations to start your day

Commit
Transform your body and your life with the power of Yes!

Begin with Yes – At Work for You
The book of workplace wisdom.

(blank page)

Paul Boynton

Author and Chief Optimist at Begin with Yes

Paul Boynton, M.A. is the author of "Begin with Yes" and several additional bestselling books on personal growth and change. His Facebook page continues to grow with fans from around the world. Paul is also President & CEO of The Moore Center, an organization serving people with developmental disabilities. He's a popular keynote presenter, webinar leader, blogger for The Huffington Post, The Good Men's Project, a past columnist for the NH Business Review and host of a radio show on Empower Radio. Paul has degrees in social work and counseling. He lives in NH with his partner Mike and their lovable pooch Toby.

Made in the USA
Middletown, DE
11 August 2018